# Kumaon

## Jewel of the Himalayas

# Kumaon
## Jewel of the Himalayas

**S. Ramesh**
**Brinda Ramesh**

*Photographs by*
Jogendra Bisht

📖 **UBSPD**
## UBS Publishers' Distributors Ltd.
New Delhi • Bangalore • Chennai
Calcutta • Patna • Kanpur • London

## UBS Publishers' Distributors Ltd.

**5 Ansari Road, New Delhi-110 002**
*Phones*: 3273601, 3266646 ● *Cable*: ALLBOOKS ●
*Fax*: 3276593, 3274261
E-mail: ubspd@gobookshopping.com ● Website: www.gobookshopping.com

**10 First Main Road, Gandhi Nagar, Bangalore-560 009**
*Phones*: 2263901, 2263902, 2253903 ● *Cable*: ALLBOOKS ●
*Fax*: 2263904 ● E-mail: ubspdbng@bgl.vsnl.net.in

**6, Sivaganga Road, Nungambakkam, Chennai-600 034**
*Phones*: 8276355, 8270189 ● *Cable*: UBSIPUB ● *Fax*: 8278920
E-mail: ubspdche@md4.vsnl.net.in

**8/1-B, Chowringhee Lane, Calcutta-700 016**
*Phones*: 2441821, 2442910, 2449473 ● *Cable*: UBSIPUBS ●
*Fax*: 2450027 ● E-mail: ubspdcal@cal.vsnl.net.in

**5 A, Rajendra Nagar, Patna-800 016**
*Phones*: 672856, 673973, 686170 ● *Cable*: UBSPUB ● *Fax*: 686169
E-mail: ubspdpat@dte2.vsnl.net.in

**80, Noronha Road, Cantonment, Kanpur-208 004**
*Phones*: 369124, 362665, 357488 ● *Fax*: 315122
E-mail: ubsknp@lw1.vsnl.net.in

***Distributors for Western India:***
**M/s Preface Books**
Unit No. 223, (2nd floor), Cama Industrial Estate,
Sun Mill Compound, Lower Parel (West), Mumbai-400 013
*Phone*: 022-4988054 ● *Telefax*: 022-4988048 ● E-mail: Preface@vsnl.com

***Overseas Contact***
**475 North Circular Road, Neasden, London NW2 7QG, UK**
*Tele*: (020) 8450-8667 ● *Fax*: (020) 8452-6612 *Attn*: UBS

© **S. Ramesh and Brinda Ramesh**

S. Ramesh and Brinda Ramesh assert the moral right to be identified as
the authors of this work

First Published **2001**

*Cover Design*: Shamli Nimbalkar

*Printed at* Imprint Solutions, Delhi

*In memory of our dear friend Khurshid*

कृष्ण चन्द्र पन्त
K.C. PANT

उपाध्यक्ष
योजना आयोग
भारत
DEPUTY CHAIRMAN
PLANNING COMMISSION
INDIA

October 31, 2000

# Foreword

With the formation of Uttaranchal State comprising of Kumaon and Garhwal regions, in November 2000, there is bound to be renewed interest in this fascinating area of our country. Sometimes remote and forbidding, but always beautiful, the Himalayas have been an area of perennial attraction to people from all over the world. The Kumaon area of Uttaranchal is one of the most attractive parts of the Western Himalayas.

It is in this background that I welcome this addition to Himalayan literature by the present authors, who are well-qualified to write on this subject. The book has covered various aspects of Kumaon in a lucid and readable manner, and should appeal not only to the general reader, but also to administrators, tourists and others interested in the Himalayas in general and Kumaon in particular.

**(K.C. PANT)**

vii

# Preface

The Himalayas have attracted considerable attention, and reasonably so, from scholars, philosophers and religious savants from times immemorial. Though travellers from all over the globe have traversed their fascinating peaks and valleys, large parts of the Himalayas have become more accessible to the tourists and other visitors with the improvements in road communications in recent years.

There are a number of books available on the Himalayas, but we feel that the reader would still be interested in a book covering the historical, geological, ecological and sociological aspects of the region. This book is about one of the most facsinating regions of the western Himalayas — Kumaon. The new Uttaranchal state comprising Kumaon and Garhwal regions came into existence in November, 2000, and we feel that this is an appropriate time for the reader to be acquainted with the captivating features of the region. This book, we hope, will be of interest for not only the general readers but also the administrators and others in public life interested in Kumaon. For us, who live in Ranikhet in the Kumaon hills, this book has been a labour of love.

We acknowledge our debt to numerous earlier books on various aspects of the Himalayas, many of which are listed in the Bibliography. A number of our friends have helped with comments, suggestions and material. We would like to specially mention Vasudha Pande, Krishna Chauhan, Dag Winje Jakobsen, Ramesh Bhatt, Devendra Bhatt, and Jogendra Bisht for their encouragement and assistance. Jogendra Bisht also contributed the photographs in the book. For the books and other material made available to us during our work, we are thankful to Dr. R.S. Tolia, Director of the Administrative Training Institute, Nainital, and Dr. Palni of the Govind Ballabh Pant Institute of Himalayan Environment and Development, Katarmal, Almora.

We are grateful to Shri K.C. Pant, a distinguished Kumaoni and Deputy Chairman of the Planning Commission, for being kind enough to write the Foreword for the book.

Ranikhet                                     **S. Ramesh**
                                             **Brinda Ramesh**

# Contents

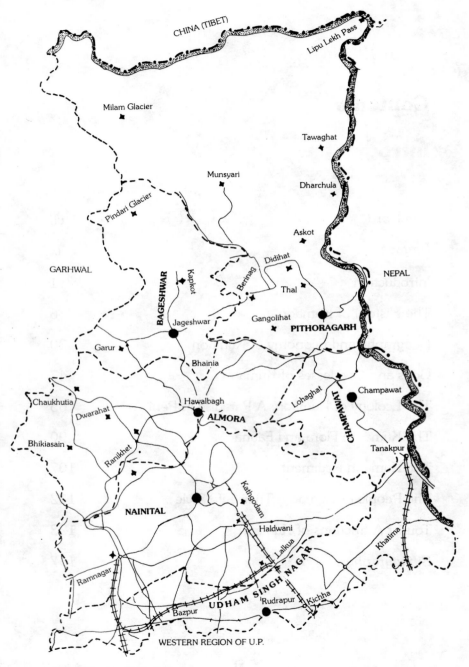

Map of Kumaun. Not to Scale

## Chapter 1

# Introduction

Kumaon and Garhwal are the two main cultural sub-regions of the area known as 'Uttarakhand' or 'Uttaranchal'. *Kumaon* is a term historically derived from the name 'Kurmanchal', which literally means 'mountain of tortoise'. This has a mythological origin as the tortoise incarnation of God Vishnu was supposed to have occurred in Champawat in the border of the Kumaon region. Originally, the term 'Kumaon Himalaya' was used to describe a much larger part of the Himalayas, extending between Sutlej river in the west and Kali river in the east, stretching over 320 kilometres. The focus of discussion in what follows is the area covered by the present administrative division of Kumaon (i.e. UP Himalaya, excluding Garhwal division), which comprises the districts of Naini Tal, Almora and Pithoragarh. Recently, three new districts, viz. Udham Singh Nagar (with Rudrapur as its headquarters), Bageshwar and Champawat have been carved out of these three districts. Most statistical and other information available is still only in respect of the undivided districts, and frequently the larger entities are referred to in the course of discussions.

The focus mainly is on hill areas of Kumaon, but there are frequent references to the Rudrapur area of the division,

1

which lies entirely in the plains though, for historical reasons, it is part of an essentially hill division.

The main objective of the authors is to introduce to the general reader one of the most captivating and important regions of the country. The Himalayan districts are important to the rest of the country, especially the vast areas of its Northern parts, from various points of view. The snow falling in the hills at higher altitudes feeds the many rivers which have their origin in the Himalayas; this, of course, is in addition to the monsoon rains. The climate of North India in many ways depends on changes in the Himalayan climate. The ice melting in the frozen glaciers also feeds the rivers which irrigate vast areas in the plains as well as provide water for many other uses. Many major hydro-electric projects in the Himalayas, present as well as potential, can provide the much-needed electricity to a power-starved country. It must be remembered that only a very small part of this power is consumed in the Himalayan region where the requirements of electricity for domestic use, agriculture and industry are still comparatively small.

Area-wise, the Uttarakhand region is larger than many Indian states. At 51,112 sq. km., it is larger than Punjab (50,362 sq.km.) Haryana (44,222 sq.km.) and Kerala (38,864 sq.km.) as well as the much smaller states of Meghalaya, Manipur, Nagaland and Tripura. The hill state of Himachal Pradesh, at 55,673 sq. km., is only slightly larger. Within the Uttarakhand region itself, Kumaon has an area of 21000 sq.km. Of course, the population density of Kumaon as well as that of Garhwal is much lower than the plains areas of Uttar Pradesh, being about one-fourth of the latter. But this figure of lower density gives a misleading picture of the ground realities as large parts of the hill areas are not cultivable (some high altitudes are not even habitable) because they are either very mountainous or snow-bound areas, or covered by forests.

Chapter 2 gives a historical background of Kumaon from ancient times to the present day. The resume of the various rulers and kingdoms in the Kumaon is necessarily selective as our account does not purport to be a detailed history of this fascinating territory.

No book on the Kumaon hills would be complete without a discussion of the economy. In Chapter 3, the problems of hill agriculture and horticulture, and the limited possibilities of industrial development, lead us to search for other possibilities of income generation for the hills. Tourism, especially ecologically sustainable tourism, is definitely high on this list. At present, the hill economy is sustained to a large extent by the remittances from the incomes earned outside the hill areas by Kumaonis working in the defence and paramilitary forces as well as other types of employment in the towns and cities in the plains. This is frequently described as the 'money order economy'. While this type of income flows into the hill areas is expected to continue, there will also be opportunities for the new Uttarakhand state to tap some of its rich hydroelectric potential in order to generate electric power. As the limited electricity consumption in the hill areas will leave a lot of surplus power for sale to the neighbouring states, this can prove to be a viable source of income for the hill state.

One interesting part of the social and cultural life of the Kumaon hills is the mythology and religious practices, both pre-Hindu as well as Hindu, which one encounters daily in these hills. Some of the stories are passed on down the generations by word of mouth, but many have been written about by foreign as well as Indian scholars. In Chapter 4, we have some of the interesting local legends and stories. Attention had been devoted to the traditions of the pre-Hindu pantheon not only because these stories may not be so readily available to the reader but also because they have a typical Kumaoni flavour.

The ecological crisis confronting the hill areas is often written about by newspaper columnists. Environmental activists and others also have spoken on this subject on many platforms. However, the real nature and extent of the ecological problems of the hill areas are often not realised. Some of these issues are presented in Chapter 5, specifically with reference to the Kumaon hills, but much of the discussion has relevance to the rest of the Himalayas as well. It is important to mention that the deforestation, soil erosion and the water crisis in the hill areas influence the conditions in the plains as well in many ways. Even the climate in the plains, especially in North India, is substantially dependent on the Himalayas. It can truly be said that if the hills sneeze, the plains shiver!

The flora and fauna of the region is the subject of Chapter 6. It must be mentioned that the bird, animal and reptile life as well as the plants and vegetation of the Kumaon hills are broadly similar to the rest of the western Himalayas, though they may differ in some respects. The discussion of flora and fauna is by no means as comprehensive or as rigorous as a serious botanist or student of wild life may desire. However, an effort has been made to give an introduction to the subject which would not only give a good idea of the plant and animal life in the Kumaon but may well stimulate interested readers to delve further into the subject.

In view of the major role played by the Kumaon Regiment in various defence operations during the last five decades and the close association of the Army with most Kumaoni families (almost every family has a serving or a retired Army man in its fold), Chapter 7 gives a brief account of the famous regiment which is an integral part of Kumaon.

The sociological background of the Kumaonis is very important in their economic and social development. The role of women in Kumaoni society is of special interest in this regard. Chapter 8 deals with these issues. It also focuses on

Mountain View from Ranikhet Club — Nandaghunti, Trisul, Maiktoli, Nanda Devi, Nanda Devi East, Nanda Khat, Nanda Kot, (left to right)

Nandakhat peak from Phurkia

Pindari glacier

Sunset on Trisul

the festivals and fairs which are such an important part of the social and cultural life of the region.

Chapter 9 deals with the tourist attractions of Kumaon. Apart from the well-known tourist spots, it gives some information on the trekking and cycling trips that can be a major attraction for the younger tourists.

The book does not attempt to deal with the various subjects mentioned above in a comprehensive fashion. Volumes have been written on various aspects of the Kumaon and the other parts of the Himalayas by many scholars. Readers who wish to acquire more knowledge on any of the subjects would do well to consult specific books on them, a select list of which is included in the bibliography.

## Chapter 2

# The History of Kumaon

What follows is based largely on the writings of classical works on the history of Kumaon and is really a resume of the main dynasties that ruled over Kumaon and the movements that affected it. The account of the kings of Kumaon is not chronologically complete as what has been attempted is to describe the more interesting of the rulers, and chronicle some of the local stories about them and their activities. Historical patterns in Kumaon (and Garhwal) are not very distinct from the history of the rest of Northern India because neither the hills nor the high Himalayas have ever been a barrier to cross-cultural movements or dynastic associations. Access to Tibet and Nepal has been almost as easy as to the north Indian plains, and has continued through the ages.

The origins of the people of the area are shrouded in ambiguity, but recently discovered artifacts now seem to point to the fact that the original inhabitants were Kols of the Mund ethnic group. (These are Palaeo-Mediterranean and Proto-Australoid ethnic sub-groups who inhabited the Deccan and migrated to the Kumaon after they were defeated by the Dravidians). The present day Shilpkars are their descendants. A mongloid group, the Kirats, were the ancestors of the tribes known as the Shaukas, Baurajis, Tharus and Boksas, now collectively labelled as the Bhotias.

At a fairly early date, a group known as the Khasas probably came in from the West. Atkinson (and several other historians after him) maintain that they were an early wave of Aryan immigrants who settled down in these hills. M.C. Joshi has a very interesting paper to the effect that the Khasas, like the Tanganas and the Kushans, probably did enter the sub-continent from the north-west at the beginning of the Christian era, but since early inscriptions do not mention them specifically, he concludes that they must initially have been numerically a very small group who entered India with their cattle and their families. Later they settled in Uttarakhand and Jammu and Kashmir state. The regular Aryan immigrants who came in later tended to look down on the Khasas, because they did not 'know Brahmins' — a phrase intended to denigrate a 'less civilised' people. Though the Khasas are supposed to have played a significant role in later Kumaoni history, there is no evidence of any existing group at present that calls itself 'Khasa'. In fact, the term is now considered pejorative.

The Kunindas are generally acknowledged to be the first rulers of Kumaon, who lived in this region from about BC 1000 to 250 AD. These dates are conjectural and the earlier one is based on a mention of a certain King Subahu in the Mahabharata. The Mahabharata dates to BC 1000 and King Subahu was a Kuninda. Excavated coins and other archaeological evidence indicate that they were pastoral in nature and worshippers of the god Shiva. The Kuninda dynasty was followed by the Paurav Varman dynasty about which few details are known, except that the dynasty lasted from 647 to 725 AD.

In the middle ages, Kumaon played host to migrants from Maharashtra, Gujarat, Karanataka, Rajasthan, Bengal, Kanyakumari and Kurukshetra, all of whom integrated totally into the local culture.

It is generally acknowledged that two main dynasties ruled over Kumaon until the British entered the region. These were the Katyuris (eighth to twelfth centry AD) and the Chands who replaced them as the dominant dynasty and are supposed to have ruled from twelfth to eighteenth century AD The dates attributed to the Katyuri regime are not really verified, and perhaps, for lack of any documentation, unverifiable. Though local tradition maintains proudly that the Katyuri kingdom extended from Sikkim in the east to Kabul in the west, and encompassed both Delhi and Rohilkhand, there is little concrete evidence to bear this out. For large periods, however, the Katyuris as well as the Chands paid homage (and taxes) to other feudatory overlords.

Around the eleventh or twelfth century AD, the downfall of the Katyuri empire began. Historian B.D. Pande ascribes this to "the curse of the god Narsingh, or to oppressions of the later descendants of the Katyuris". It is said that King Vir Dev, the last of the dynasty, earned the hatred of his subjects by taxing them cruelly. As there were no tax laws at that time, the king just picked up whatever he wanted from the homes of his subjects, including beautiful children, whom he then used as slaves. To compound his crimes against god and man, he then married his maternal aunt, thereby not only outraging public sentiment, but immortalising himself in Kumaoni folklore by providing the theme for a Kumaoni folk song *Mami tile dharo bole*.

His iniquities, debaucheries and oppression became so great and unbearable that two of his palanquin bearers decided to martyr themselves for the sake of their fellowmen. While carrying him to the village in a *dandi*, they jumped off the mountain path into a ravine, thus destroying not only the tyrant but themselves as well.

After his death, civil war ensued and the immense Katyuri empire disintegrated. Family members and provincial governors who had been appointed by the Katyuris carved out principalities for themselves. The kings of Garhwal, who at one stage had been feudatory lords under them, stopped paying their taxes and became independent. For some time after the disintegration of the Katyuri empire, Kumaon was subjugated by the Mallas of Western Nepal.

## The Chands

It is believed that, displeased by the disintegration of the empire and the consequent warfare among the Katyuris and the feudatory Khasa chieftains, a delegation from Kumaon went to Prayag and requested Prince Som Chand of the Lunar dynasty to help them. He was brought to Kumaon, inculcated into the customs and rituals of the region, married to a Katyuri princess and established on the throne. This became an established matrimonial custom, and for many years after the Chands continued to marry girls from the families of the Palas, Sahis, Manrals and Rajwars of Askot. (All these families are considered to be descendants of the Katyuris). But the daughters of the Chands were always married off elsewhere. The date of Som Chand's accession is shrouded in mystery, with historians giving such widely separated dates as 685 or 700 AD, and according to other traditions, as late as 1178 AD or 1208 AD. Though it is popularly supposed that Som Chand was the first of the Chand kings, modern historians have now advanced the theory that this position can really be claimed by Thohar Chand, who was brought from Jhusi when he was 16 or 17 years old around 1261 AD.

When Som Chand became the 'king' and established himself in Champawat, he was only a small feudatory princeling, a *zamindar* paying taxes to the king of Doti. But in the twenty-one years of his rule, he enlarged his kingdom extensively and the whole of Kali Kumaon came under his rule. There seems to have been a period subsequent to this when the Chands lost control over Kali Kumaon to the Khasa

kings and had to flee to Nepal Tarai. In the meantime,
disaffected courtiers repeatedly invited the Katyuris to return,
but they were unable to do so because of disunity among
them. The Khasa rule is supposed to have lasted for two
hundred years, during which period their kingdom extended
from Kashmir to Assam and included Rajasthan and
Vindhyachal. No authenticated facts about this period are
available though some of the Khasa rulers were thought to
be Buddhists.

In the early part of the eleventh century — 1065 AD or
thereabouts — the people of Kali Kumaon, by now fed up
with their Khasa rulers, recalled Vir Chand from Nepal and
the Chands resumed control over Champawat again. Once
again we find that little information is available about
subsequent rulers until Jnana Chand (also known as Gyan
Chand, 1374–1419) became the king. He ruled for forty-five
years. The Chands always maintained excellent relations with
the Mughal emperors, and Jnana Chand paid a visit to the
court of Muhammad ibn Tughlaq, to ask for the return of
Tarai Bhabar, which had been annexed by the Nawab of
Rohilkhand. During this visit, Jnana Chand accompanied the
emperor on a *shikar* and bagged an eagle carrying a snake
in its beak with his bow. The emperor was so impressed by
his prowess that he immediately issued an order that the Tarai
Bhabar up to the Bhagirathi Ganga would henceforth be
restored to the King of Kumaon. He also gave Jnana Chand
the title of Garud Gyan Chand.

Soon after, however, the Nawab of Sambhal occupied the
Tarai and Gyan Chand ordered the commander of his army,
Sardar Nilu Kathayat, to retake the area. This he did with
great courage and resource, and was rewarded for his pains.
But as is inevitable with kings, courts and courtiers, this
provoked the envy of another influential courtier, Jassa
Kamlekhi, who persuaded Gyan Chand to send Nilu Kathayat
as governor of Tarai Bhabar. Nilu rushed to the court to
protest, for the hill people did not like to live in the unhealthy

Tarai. Jassa convinced the king that this was an act of grave insubordination, and so the king refused to meet Nilu, who returned home very demoralised. His wife then persuaded him to send his two young sons to the court to intercede for him. Again instigated by Jassa, the king had the two young children blinded. Justly incensed, Nilu then attacked the palace with his men. The king and Jassa then fled into the jungle, where they were found by Nilu. Nilu killed Jassa, but spared the life of Gyan Chand, saying it would bring dishonour to his family if he raised his hand against his ruler and master. The king pretended to make his peace with Nilu, but subsequently had Nilu assassinated. This treacherous act brought so much disrepute upon the Chand dynasty that Garud Gyan Chand's grand son Udyan Chand spent his brief reign building temples and giving alms to expiate his grandfather's sin.

During this period of Kumaoni history, the Chands were not the only dynasty ruling the area. The Katyuris and the Mankotis also had substantial holdings, and wars among them were inevitable and frequent.

King Vikram Chand (1433–1437) spent the early part of his reign giving alms and building temples in order to make up for the sins and shortcomings of Garud Gyan Chand, but in mid-life, tired of piety and giving up good deeds and administration, he gave himself up to personal pleasure and indulgence. This antagonised not only the general public but also his courtiers. The Kumaonis, led by his own nephew Bharati, revolted against him. Bharati asked for help in this war from the leader of the Khasa clan, one Shand Karayat. Vikram Chand retaliated in the gory manner of those times by seizing the son of Shand Karayat and having him killed by plastering him up in a brick wall. Shand Karayat then went to Bharati Chand's assistance, and Vikram Chand was ousted and Bharati Chand was put on the throne (1437–1450).

Before the ascension of Bharati Chand, the Chands had paid taxes to the Doti kings, who were their feudatory overlords, but Bharati Chand stopped paying these taxes, broke away altogether and waged war against the Dotis for twelve years. After the Chands became independent, Bharati Chand abdicated in favour of his son Ratna Chand (1450–1488). Ratna Chand attributed the good fortunes of his family to the *shivlinga* at Jageshwar, and showed his gratitude by donating villages and giving alms for the maintenance of the temple. He then enlarged the boundaries of the kingdom and, most important of all, made a kind of land settlement, the first of its kind in this area.

Jaidan Kirat was appointed the first settlement officer, and he did an efficient job of maintaining land records. But since his activities made it impossible for people to hide their wealth, he became unpopular. So, when he went away to an adjoining area to collect land revenue, his enemies told his wife that he had died, and persuaded her to become *sati*. To gladden her dead husband's heart in the next world, they encouraged her to take with her to the funeral pyre all his settlement records. Since Jaidan Kiral died shortly afterwards, the attempt to create some sort of revenue record system came to an end.

During the reign of King Kirati Chand (1488–1503), the Katyuris were finally divested of the lands over which they had ruled, and they retired to Salt, building a fort at Manila. Kirat Chand then extended his kingdom to include Baramandal, Pali and Manila. Though the Katyuris were now reduced to the status of *zamindars*, they were permitted to live peacefully at Manila.

King Bhisham Chand (1555–1560) shifted the capital of the Chand empire from Champawat to Khagmarkot and laid the foundation stone of Alamnagar, which later came to be called Almora. Rudra Chand was king from 1568 to 1597. During his reign Hussain Khan Tukadiya invaded Kumaon twice. Emperor Akbar sent for him in order to reprimand him, but he died on his way to Delhi, and Rudra Chand re-established control over the Tarai region which Hussain Khan Tukadia had annexed. The town of Rudrapur was then founded by Rudra Chand. A King Bruce-like legend attaches to his name. Foiled repeatedly in his attempt to take Sira in Garhwal, he saw a spider attempting to spin a web. It failed six times but succeeded in the seventh attempt. Inspired, Rudra Chand tried again and again and, like the spider, he succeeded in the seventh attempt. His court was a haven for renowned Sanskrit scholars and he himself is reputed to have composed two Sanskrit works, *Shyen Shastra* and *Dharm Nirnay*.

King Laxmi Chand ( 1597–1621) imposed such heavy taxes on cultivable land that the public, especially the people of Bageshwar, began to grow vegetables on the roof tops. To his credit it must be said that when he was told why they had recourse to such stratagems, he promptly withdrew these extortionate taxes, but the custom prevails to this day. Laxmi Chand was also responsible for instituting a local custom or festival that is still celebrated. He invaded Garhwal seven times but was repulsed each time. The eighth attempt was made after 1602. This time he won a small victory. It was not particularly notable, but to convey the news to Almora, small fires of wood and grass were lighted on the hill tops. This is still done on *ashvin sankranti* to commemorate the victory. The festival is called *Khatduva* and heralds the advent of winter.

The Chand kingdom began to  decline after Laxmi Chand. His son Vijay Chand succeeded him, but gave himself up to debauchery and was assassinated by the kitchen staff.

By the time Baz Bahadur Chand (1638–1678) came to the throne, the Chands had started fighting among themselves, as a result of which parts of the kingdom had been snatched away by other chieftains. In return for assisting Emperor Aurangzeb against the Raja of Garhwal, Baz Bahadur was assisted by the Mughal emperor to retake and consolidate his rule over these territories, and was called the 'Zamindar of Kumaon'. He is reputed to have brought away the image of the goddess Nanda Devi from Garhwal and installed it in Malla Mahal, where it stayed till Commissioner Traill shifted it to its present abode in Almora after the British takeover of Kumaon. Baz Bahadur was also responsible for winning over the remnants of the Katyuris by giving them land and court responsibilities — and, when required, by destroying their fortresses. He also built the temples of Bhimeshwar in Bhimtal and the Sun temple of Katarmal. The latter, incidentally, was ranked as an architectural wonder as important as the Sun temple of Konark, till it was despoiled and the main image stolen. The stable door was locked after the horse was stolen, and the elaborately carved doors of the temples have now been removed to the National Museum in Delhi.

Baz Bahadur was a wise  man and a good king, but in time, he too fell prey to the machinations of his courtiers. He blinded and killed hundreds of his officers on the advice of one of them whom he trusted far beyond his deserts. This advisor piled up two heaps of rice, and the courtiers were asked to touch one of them. Those who touched the heap designated `bad' were punished, those who touched the `good' heap were rewarded. Consequently, Baz Bahadur earned much illwill and fell into disrepute. Fortunately for him, he was brought back to his senses by a favourite attendant called Sri Sundar Lal Bhandari, but he also provided the inspiration for a famous Kumaoni proverb — 'when someone is over eighty years old, he has no wisdom left'.

On the whole, Baz Bahadur was a good king, and his reign was a good one for his subjects, but his end was pathetic. He became extremely suspicious, dismissed all his servants, and died alone and in great pain.

King Devi Chand (1720–1726) is supposed to have been born to fulfill the prophesy of a Brahmin who came to his father Jagat Chand, demanding the sum of Rs. 10,000 in order to pursue his studies. When he was offered a more reasonable amount, he refused it and went away to Banaras declaring that he would ensure that, through his special powers, the Chand treasury was depleted. Then he committed suicide.

Devi Chand was born after this incident. As soon as he came to the throne, he continued the usual war with Garhwal according to the traditions established by his predecessors. But then he saw the enormous amounts of money in the treasury, and his thoughts turned away from dreams of conquest. He started to spend the money, initially by giving lavish gifts to his courtiers. But soon his excesses became quite eccentric. Since he could not fulfill his ambition of conquering Srinagar in Garhwal, he named a peak near Hawalbagh as 'Srinagar'. He then proceeded to 'capture' it. To celebrate his 'victory' he had the entire hillside carpeted. He then said the trees were feeling cold, and had them covered in cloth of gold. He renamed the hilltop Fatehpur, and then entered it with great pomp and show. Quite naturally, his long suffering public decided he was a reincarnation of the Brahmin who had been born again to despoil the kingdom. His courtiers took advantage of his madness, and grabbed whatever was left in the treasury. Then they instigated him to attack the Mughal emperor at Delhi. One of his main advisors was his Afghan commander, Daud Khan.

Devi Chand set off towards Nagina on his way to Delhi, but here he was deserted by Daud Khan, who went over to the enemy. In the meantime, the King of Garhwal attacked Kumaon. In the middle of the campaign, Devi Chand abandoned the wars he had initiated and went away to Devipur, where he gave himself up to a life of pleasure. His mad career came to an end when he was murdered by two of his exasperated courtiers.

Manak Chand Gauda Bisht and his son Puran Mal Bisht then took charge of the kingdom, and installed Ajit Chand

(son of King Narpat Singh of Rohilkhand) in 1726 as a
puppet king. They took back all the gifts that Devi Chand
had given to his courtiers, and behaved with great arrogance
and cruelty. When Ajit Chand protested, they killed him in
1729 and demanded of King Narpat Singh that he send his
second son to rule over Kumaon. King Narpat Singh is
supposed to have replied, "My sons are not goats to be
repeatedly offered by you as victims to the goddess of
Kumaon". Puran Mal Bisht then installed an eighteen-day old
child on the throne, claiming that he was the son of Ajit
Chand. Popular opinion maintained that it was his own
illegitimate child.

The other courtiers did not approve of this and the
Fartyals and Mahars decided to put one Kalyan Chand on
the throne. Though he was the son of Bar Bahadur Chand
he had been brought up as a labourer and was illiterate.

King Kalyan Chand (1729–1747) started his reign by
putting Puranmal and his father Manikchand Gaida Bisht to
death. He then tried to turn his mind to affairs of state, but
after he had built a four-storeyed mansion, he lost interest
in the work of governance. He then turned to bloodshed.
Having killed the Bishts he tried to kill all the Chands and
Rautelas in the Kumaon so that the princely line was
eliminated and he could never be replaced. His passion for
extermination became so extreme that if anyone wanted to
get rid of a rival in the village, he just had to inform the king's
emissaries that he was a Chand or a Rautela. He could then
lay hands on the dead man's property, after duly gratifying
the king's officials.

Kalyan Chand was completely manipulated by his
courtiers and officials. Once, he was informed by his chief
of police that a group of Brahmins and *zamindars* were
plotting to kill him and to invite the son of Sawai Jai Singh
of Jaipur to ascend the throne. Without asking for proof, the
king had all the accused Brahmins blinded. There were so
many of them that, it is said, seven large vessels were filled

with their eyeballs. The implicated *zamindars* were killed, and their bodies were left on the banks of the river to be eaten by jackals, kites and crows.

Himmat Singh Rautela, who had fled Kumaon when Kalyan Singh started killing Chands and Rautelas, was now approached by dissaffected Kumaonis. At their request he collected an army and attacked Kumaon, but he was defeated by the chieftain of Kashipur. He then took shelter with the Rohilla Nawab of Rampur.

Towards the latter part of his reign, Kalyan Chand repented of his bloodthirsty ways and tried to make reparation by giving costly presents, money, court appointments and gifts of land to the successors of those he had killed. However, his repentance was obviously not complete. Nor did it herald a genuine desire to mend his ways, for at the same time, he had Himmat Singh Rautela assassinated. The Nawab of Rampur took this opportunity to attack Kumaon. Ostensibly, he wanted to avenge the murder of his guest, but in reality, he wished to annex the hill kingdom, and use it as a refuge, in case his disputes with the Mughal Emperor at Delhi became serious. The Nawab of Awadh also annexed some parts of the Tarai at this time.

In 1743–44, the Rohilla army defeated Kalyan Chand's army, led by his General Shivdeo Joshi, at Rudrapur and marched into Almora. Kalyan Chand took shelter in Garhwal. The Rohillas demolished houses and temples, and plundered the area. Local legend has it that only the temple complex at Jageshwar escaped being looted — and this was because swarms of bees attacked the Rohilla troops as they marched towards it. The Rohillas also set fire to government records, which is why it is now impossible to get authentic information about the early history of Kumaon.

However, once again nature succeeded where the army could not. The Rohilla army could not withstand the cold Almora winter and many soldiers sickened and died. The King of Garhwal came to the assistance of his Kumaoni

counterpart and joined him in attacking the Rohillas. Though
the Rohillas were not defeated, they had had enough of
Kumaon and readily came to terms with the King of Garhwal.
The latter agreed to pay them a sum of three lakh rupees
on behalf of Kalyan Chand, and the Rohillas abandoned
Almora and returned to Rampur, to the disgust of the Nawab
Ali Muhammad Shah who now lost his mountain retreat. In
1745, the small garrison that the Rohillas had left behind
was also forced to abandon the hills. Both Kalyan Chand and
Ali Muhammad Shah died in 1748.

Kalyan Chand's successor was his son Deep Chand
(1748-1777), a mild, gentle, kind and generous man, much
given to prayer and to donating alms to temples. He was
not very interested in the work of administration and so his
kingdom was very competently looked after for him by Shib
Deo. The Raja of Garhwal attacked Kumaon and was
repulsed, but Shib Deo was murdered at the instigation of
the Fartyals. Mohan Singh, a cousin of Deep Chand, assumed
charge of the army. A confusing period of Kumaoni history
followed, marked by extreme violence. Mohan Singh became
the prime minister, but court intrigue ousted him for a while,
and replaced him with Parmanand Bisht and Harak Deb Joshi
But political jockeying for positions continued and subsequently when Mohan Singh found himself once more in
the ascendance, he had Parmanand Bisht killed. However,
he himself was forced to flee the kingdom again, and during
this period Harak Deb Joshi was appointed as prime minister
and head of the armed forces.

However, Mohan Singh returned to Kumaon yet again,
this time with the not very enthusiastic consent of Harak Deb
and Jaikishan Joshi (son of Shib Deo), who were handling
the affairs of the kingdom jointly at this period. Shortly
afterwards, Mohan Singh instigated Jaikishan to enter into a
battle for the possession of Kashipur. At the same time, he
assisted the opposing army too, and had Jaikishan defeated
and then killed. He then took over the reins of the kingdom,

and condemned Harak Deb to perpetual imprisonment. Mohan Singh then had himself proclaimed king in 1777 taking the title of Mohan Chand.

In 1779, the Raja of Garhwal attacked Kumaon, and Mohan Singh fled to Rampur. As a result, a Garhwali ascended the throne of Almora. This was Pradhaman Sah who was now called Pradhaman Chand. His brother Parakram Sah ruled in Srinagar, Garhwal, and Pradhaman Sah, the King in Almora played an active part in the further affairs of Kumaon, sometimes supporting each other and at other times being at daggers drawn.

Harak Deb, who was released from prison, seems to have been held in respect and regard by the Garhwali rulers of Almora. In the meantime, Mohan Singh, who had fled from the hills towards Banaras, linked his lot with a group of fighting mendicants and, with their help, invaded Kumaon again. They were promised the privilege of looting the wealth of Almora as recompense. They infiltrated into the hills, pretending to be pilgrims to Badrinath, but were discovered and defeated. In the meantime, the Raja of Garhwal Parakram Sah, tried to persuade his younger brother who ruled in Almora that he had the right to rule both the kingdoms because of his seniority in age. Harak Deb Joshi went to Garhwal in order to settle matters on behalf of Pradhaman Sah of Kumaon but, when Parakram Sah refused to meet him, he attacked Garhwal with the help of a strong force that he had taken with him and Kumaonis captured Srinagar, the capital of Garhwal. This raid into Garhwal is still called 'the *Joshiyana*'. Subsequently, Harak Deb did everything he could to strengthen the position of Pradhaman Sah in Almora, but with scant success for the populace had little use for a king whose heart, they thought, was in Srinagar. Pradhaman Shah was then attacked by Mohan Singh from the east, Nandram from the Tarai and the Garhwalis from the west. His army, commanded by Harak Deb was defeated and fled.

Mohan Singh installed himself on the throne of Kumaon again, but this time the state exchequer was depleted, and he tried to raise money by plundering the countryside. A disaffected populace made it easy for Harak Deb to invade Kumaon once more, this time with considerable success. Mohan Singh was captured and killed in 1788 AD.

Confusion prevailed once again in Kumaon. Parakram Sah and Pradhaman Sah added to it by interfering in Kumaoni affairs, usually on opposite sides. One supported Harak Deb in his war on behalf of Sib Chand, the new king of Kumaon, and the other threw in his lot with Lal Singh, the brother of Mohan Singh.

In 1790, the Gorkha army entered Kumaon and took possession of Almora, supported very unpatriotically by Harak Deb, who was by this time fed up with local politics and with the treatment meted out to him personally. However, it did not take him long to get fed up with the Gorkhas too, and he retired to Srinagar, Garhwal.

In 1791, the Gorkhas introduced the first settlement of land revenue. Kazi Nar Shah became the administrator of Kumaon in 1793, and was noted for his cruelty and harshness. One of his most reprehensible acts was to make a census of Nepalese mercenaries who had settled in Kumaon, and then have them systematically murdered as he suspected their loyalty. The massacre took place on a Tuesday night and, after that, any act of treachery or villainy was referred to as *mangal ki raat*.

The Gorkhas conquered Garhwal in 1803. Their administration of this region was marked by such extremes of harshness and tyranny that the Kumaonis were probably slightly better off — but only marginally so.

When Bam Shah became the governor, the Kumaoni lot became definitely better than that of the people of Garhwal. Large numbers of Kumaonis were inducted into the Nepalese army, though their battalions were maintained separately.

Himalayan view from authors' house in Ranikhet

Pualidwar Peak from Dhakuri Pass on the way to Pindari glacier

On the way to Pindari glacier

Nanda Devi peak — the flat top in the middle of the range

The Gorkhas evolved a highly personalised system of administering justice, which contributed to the sufferings of the populace that they governed. Civil and petty criminal cases were looked into by the commandant of the troops who was in charge of that particular area while more serious cases were to be decided by the civil governor. But usually deputies decided these cases, and the law they administered was that of trial by ordeal, especially where there was no eyewitness.

Three forms of ordeal were commonly employed — (a) the accused was made to carry a bar of red hot iron for a certain distance, (b) the hands of the accused were plunged into burning oil and, as in the case of the former ordeal, the evidence of innocence was that not much harm resulted, and (c) the accused was weighed against a number of stones, which were carefully sealed; he was weighed again the next morning, and if he weighed more, he was presumed innocent. The *mahant* of a certain temple in Garhwal was forced to undergo the ordeal by oil and, because he was severely burnt, he had to pay a huge fine.

In civil litigation too, equally irrational practices were followed. Sometimes, the names of rival claimants were written on pieces of paper and then placed before the idol in a temple. The slip picked up by the temple priest decided who was the winner of the suit. Sometimes, litigants — non-swimmers — were thrown into water, and the one who survived automatically became the winner. Or the accused would be forced to stand under water while a friend ran the distance of an arrow shot and returned. If the accused survived, he was acquitted. Ordeal by poison was also employed, the survivor automatically emerging the victor. The Chand rulers rarely condemned criminals to death, but the Gorkhalis favoured the death penalty frequently. However, it must be pointed out that the Gorkhas were not exceptionally cruel to the Kumaonis. These methods of administering justice prevailed in their own territories also. However, their harshness was such that the local public soon grew to hate them.

In the meantime, the Gorkhas were becoming increasingly bold in their incursions into British territory, especially near Gorakhpur. Initially, the British reacted with moderation. This was interpreted as weakness by the Nepalese, and the provocation became more and more acute. Finally, in November 1814, the British army attacked the Nepalese army simultaneously on several fronts. The Nepalese were heavily outnumbered, but some of the British commanders were so incompetent that the Nepalese managed to give a good account of themselves. Their defence of Kalanga near Dehra in Garhwal, where they held out valiantly under actrocious conditions, was so heroic that it won them the respect of their enemies.

Meanwhile, Lord Hastings, the Governor General of India, decided that, for economic and political reasons, Kumaon and Garhwal should be annexed to British territories. Harak Deb Joshi, hereditary minister of the Chand *rajas*, now totally fed up with the Gorkhas, cast in his lot with the Honourable E. Gardner of the Bengal Civil Service, who had been sent to Moradabad to oversee the annexation. Finding Bam Sah, the Nepalese Governor of Almora, not amenable to negotiation, the British troops attacked, entering Kumaon via Dhikuli near Kosi in February 1815. The Gorkhas, entrenched in Kumpur near Ranikhet held out valiantly and for a considerable length of time even though the detachment was very small, But Gardner advanced towards Almora via Katarmal. The success of the British can be attributed not only to superior numbers and good generalship, but also to the tremendous support extended to the British by the local people, now thoroughly disgusted by 25 years of tyrannical Gorkha rule. Harak Deb Joshi played a large part in persuading the Kumaonis to assist the British.

In the meantime, the eastern flank of Kumaon was attacked by Captain Hearsey, who took Champawat. He was also greatly helped by Kumaoni levies who flocked to the British banner when urged to do so by Harak Deb Joshi. The

British suffered a temporary setback when Capt Hearsey was defeated and captured by the Gorkha General Hastidal, who immediately reoccupied Almora, but this time Lord Hastings decided to send in a part of the regular British Army to assist Colonel Edward Gardner in his work of annexation. The Gorkhas were in no position to oppose a large British force. Their numbers were not large enough, and they were handicapped by the acute local hostility that they faced.

Colonel Nicholls, in charge of the regular British forces, moved into Kumaon and assumed command not only of the army, but also of civil affairs. Soon after, the Gorkha forces under Hastidal were resoundingly defeated at Gananath, fifteen miles north of Almora. Hastidal was killed, but the British retreated to Katarmal. However, they lost no time in advancing to the town of Almora. On 27 April, 1815, after very heavy fighting, Bam Shah, the Governor of Kumaon agreed to evacuate Kumaon, and retreat with the Nepalese forces across the Kali. A treaty to this effect was signed and Colonel Gardner issued a proclamation declaring that the province of Kumaon was attached to the British provinces, and invited the local people of Almora who had fled from their homes during the war to return.

Edward Gardner was then appointed Commissioner for Kumaon, and agent to the Governor General. G.W. Traill was appointed his assistant. Gardner's first task was to formalise the delineation of the borders between Kumaon and Nepal, and his attention was primarily directed to this project. Soon after this work was done, he was appointed political agent to the court of Kathmandu, where he took over in 1816, handing over charge of Kumaon to G.W. Traill. It must be remembered that the British administration of Indian territories was at this time under the East India Company, which had its headquarters in Calcutta, and Gardner and Traill were both company employees. However, two years before the annexation of Kumaon-Garhwal, the British Parliament, while leaving the governance of the country in the hands of

the company for another 20 years, had abolished the
company's monopoly of the India trade and assigned to the
Crown the power of appointing the Governor General,
Governors, and the Commander-in-Chief. Lord Francis
Hastings became the Governor General under this
arrangement. He also continued to be the Commander-in-
Chief. In the initial years the administrative history of Kumaon
is divided into three periods — Kumaon under Traill, Kumaon
under Batten and Kumaon under Ramsay. Under Traill, the
administration was essentially paternal, despotic and personal.
Traill turned out to be the most remarkable of the British
administrators of this region, and also the most popular. He
spent 20 of his 25 years of service in Kumaon and
distinguished himself by his acute sensitivity to the needs and
desires of his people. The Bishop of Calcutta wrote:

> It is pleasing to see on how apparent good terms
> Mr. Traill is with all these people. Their manner in talking
> to him is erect, open and cheerful, like persons who are
> addressing a superior whom they love, and with whom
> they are in habits of easy, though respectful, intercourse.

The traveller P. Barron, (known as the 'pilgrim') who
'discovered' Naini Tal for the Europeans, was surprised to
find that his native guides claimed to be totally ignorant of
the existence of an area of such surpassing beauty. He came
to the conclusion that they were wilfully misleading him, and
that they were being encouraged in their behaviour by Traill

> ... the late Commissioner of Kumaon, who is said to have
> paid a visit to this lake many years ago, and, it is well
> known, possessed the most extraordinary influence
> among the natives of the hills and entertained peculiarly
> illiberal ideas regarding the influx of European visitors into
> the province.[32]

Traill initiated the first revenue and police administrative machinery in Kumaon-Garhwal and ensured that it was distinct from that of the plains and more suited to *pahari* conditions. Subsequent administrators, after a number of experiments that brought considerable hardship on the the poor peasantry of the area, decided that the system evolved by Traill was by far the most suited to the area.

In fact, 110 years later, Philip Mason (Woodruff), then Deputy Commissioner of Pauri Garhwal in the late 1930s was to write, "...more than a hundred years later the people of the hills would set finality on discussion with the words: It was so in Traill Sahib's day"

There was (and still is) a considerable shortage of labour in the hills, which made it difficult for troop movement and civilian tourist travel. The government had passed orders that the collectors of the various districts were empowered to hire porters for all such movement. This order was vehemently disliked not only by all *paharis* but by Traill himself. His first act as commissioner was to prohibit all civil and military travellers from pressing hill porters to carry their personal baggage or perform any other service for them. Instead, they were asked to engage coolies from the plains to do these jobs. This act went a long way toward endearing him to the local populace, for they hated coolie duties and this provoked them into migrating to Bhabar or Nepalese territories. He was not able to abolish the coolie system entirely, for the army required considerable help to move its commissariat, but Traill organised deployments of mules and also established rules by which each village had to provide one porter for every four houses, and these were to be pressed into service by rotation. His orders as regards porters caused a lot of heart-burning between the civil and military authorities over the matter of providing labour to the latter, and Traill did his best to solve matters by raising the rates paid to the porters and ensuring that only a limited number were to be organised from the local villages. To their credit it must be admitted that the Kumaonis appreciated the efforts Traill made to spare them this hateful duty. Their dislike of the system is made clear by the fact that the first act of civil disobedience during the independence movement on the hills was when the coolie registers were thrown into the river at Bageshwar by the freedom fighter, B.D. Pande in 1921. Traill was also responsible for the construction of many roads and bridle paths which he intended to open up the interior to trade. He did not think much of road building to facilitate military movement, but he was very interested in helping the economic development of these areas, and many of his roads were aimed at facilitating commerce with Tibet. To this end, he travelled extensively in the hills, and Traill's Pass, which connects Pindari and Milam glaciers, has been named after him to commemorate a famous journey that he made over the area during the course of which he lost his vision because of snow blindness. He was also responsible for the construction of several bridges in the area — on the Almora Bamoura road, over the Ramganga near Rameshwar, the Kosi at Hawalbagh, over the Saryu and Senril on the Almora Lohaghat Road, and over the Ramganga on the Pithoragarh road. These were all iron suspension bridges. When Traill left in 1835, after twenty years of treating Kumaon as his own personal fiefdom, there followed a period of uncertainty. Atkinson quotes Bird as saying:

> The system of government had been framed to suit the particular character and scope of one individual.... Traill left the province orderly, prosperous and comparatively civilized, but his machinery was not easily worked by another hand. There was no law, and the law-giver had been withdrawn.[5]

When Batten, at that time Assistant Commissioner of Garhwal, took over, he began by enforcing a system of codes and rules.

The commissioners who succeeded Traill — Gowan, Lushington, Batten — were largely involved in consolidating

British gains in Kumaon-Garhwal, establishing a proper system of revenue administration (administering law and order was never a problem in the area), ensuring the aboltion of slavery and the establishment of some kind of system of medical aid which would look after the local population when it was overwhelmed by epidemics of plague, cholera and smallpox. The aim of the British was to introduce British administration and justice into Kumaon, and they did this. Revenue assessment and settlement of land disputes were introduced, largely along the lines that had been introduced in the plains.

Twenty years after Traill left Sir Henry Ramsay became Commissioner Kumaon, and then, according to Bird:

> ... we see the two currents blended. The personal sway and unhampered autocracy of the first era combining with the orderly procedure and observance of fixed rules and principles which was the chief feature of the second.

He was responsible for the proper settlement of land records in the Kumaon, and for evolving a specialised system of revenue records and tax structures for hill areas, as he had no hesitation in discarding general instructions that were sent to him from the headquarters of the United Provinces, saying they were 'not suitable for Kumaon'. So successful was Ramsay as an administrator that he was popularly known as 'the king of the Kumaon'.

In 1839, what was originally called Kumaon but which included Garhwal also, was divided into the two provinces of Kumaon and Garhwal. The Tarai was formed as a new district in 1842, and in 1892 there was yet another reorganization. The new districts thus formed were Almora, Nainital and British Garhwal. The railroad was extended to Kathgodam in 1884, and Ramnagar was linked to Moradabad in 1907. Initially, the interior was linked to the railhead only by cart tracks, and some literature of the period refers interestingly to the families of 'summering' troops and army officers being conveyed to the hill stations of Almora, Nainital and Ranikhet in bullock carts or *dolis*. But in 1915, motor vehicles began to ply from Kathgodam to Nainital and, in 1920, from Kathgodam to Almora.

The Indian independence movement did not create the same turmoil in Kumaon as it did in the plains. The revolt of 1857, for instance, did not touch the hills, as the much loved and respected Sir Henry Ramsay was the commissioner of Kumaon at the time. However, by the beginning of the twentieth century, the national movement began to percolate up into the mountains. Newspapers like *Almora Akhbar* and *Shakti* began to criticise the British.

For decades, the forest department had followed a policy of conservation of forests without exploitation, a policy initiated by Ramsay, who was also the first conservator of forests. But the local population depended (and continues to depend) on the forests for fodder, fuel and grazing. In 1917, G.B. Pant, at that time Secretary of the Kumaon Association, led an agitation which led to the formation of the Kumaon Forest Committee in 1930. The committee framed policies which enabled the villagers to use forest products while at the same time helping to maintain and protect the forests.

The Kumaon Parishad was formed in 1916. Its aim was to rouse social political and cultural awareness among the people. It had among its earliest members people like Govind Ballabh Pant, Prem Ballabh Pande, Lala Indralal Shah, Thakur Mohan Singh Damdamwal, Badri Datt Pande and others. Their initial thrust was against certain British customs which the local people had begun to hate. *Kuli begar*, for instance, meant that British officers on tour had to be served free by the local people. *Kuli utaar* required the local populace to provide porters for the transportation of their men and materials, and though payment was to be made for this, it very often was not. *Kuli bardyash* meant that rations were to be supplied free to touring officers. These three customs were vehemently opposed by the Parishad at its Haldwani session in 1920 under Tara Datt Gairola. The forest policy was also criticised. In 1919, G.B. Pant launched an agitation under the aegis of the Parishad against the Rowlatt Act.

On 12 and 13 of January 1921, a movement was launched at Bageshwar by Badri Datt Pande, Har Govind Pant and Chiranji Lal against *Kuli utaar begar*, and *bardayash*. The climax of the agitation was reached when Badri Datt Pande dramatically threw the registers containing the names of the *kulis* into the Saryu River. Mahatma Gandhi described this as a bloodless revolution (*Shakti* 26 January 1925). The Quit India movement stirred the rural masses of Kumaon and firing was resorted to on two occasions in Salt and Deoghat. The two movements demanding abolition of *begar* and restitution of natural forest rights became part of the movement for independence in the Kumaon.

After India's independence in 1947, Kumaon and Garhwal were officially merged with the state of Uttar Pradesh, but in several respects their individuality was preserved. For instance, their systems of revenue and police administration are distinctive and different from that prevailing in the plains. However, since opportunities for employment are minimal in the hill areas, there was considerable discontent, and this fuelled the demand for a separate hill state.

*Chapter 3*

# Geography and Economy of Kumaon

## Introduction

With a length of 2500 km. and widths ranging from 40 to 250 km., the Himalayas, one of the youngest and certainly one of the greatest mountain systems in the world, occupy a vast area of over 500,000 sq. km. from east to west and form a natural border for the Indian sub-continent. Of this, the 'Kumaon Himalaya' extends over 320 km., from Sutlej in the west to Kali in the east. Nanda Devi is the highest peak in these ranges. The Gangotri, Pindari and the Milam glaciers as well as major river systems of India have their sources here. The part of the Himalayas which falls within the state of Uttar Pradesh consists of Garhwal and Kumaon regions. The Kumaon region or division is an administrative unit in Uttar Pradesh to be distinguished from the much wider 'Kumaon Himalaya'.

The Himalayas are also often divided into three broad regions — the western Himalaya consisting of Jammu and Kashmir and Himachal Pradesh, the central Himalaya consisting of Kumaon and Garhwal divisions, and the eastern Himalaya comprising the states of Sikkim, Manipur, Tripura, Arunachal Pradesh, Nagaland, Mizoram and the hill areas of Assam and West Bengal. The central, or UP Himalaya, often referred to as 'Uttaranchal' or 'Uttarakhand', consists of two administrative divisions, Garhwal and Kumaon, with which we are concerned here. Kumaon division comprised till recently of the three districts: Almora, Nainital and Pithoragarh. The new districts of Bageshwar, Udham Singh Nagar and Champawat have been carved from these districts. But most of the statistical and other data are available in respect of the original three districts of Almora, Nainital and Pithoragarh, and frequently we shall refer to the old (larger) districts in the course of our discussion. When we talk of 'Kumaon' in this book , we are referring to the Kumaon division of UP.

The total area of Uttaranchal is 51,125 sq. km. which is about 17 per cent of the land area of Uttar Pradesh. The population in 1991 (the latest census figures) was about 58 lakh, i.e. about 4 per cent of UP's population. The population of the original three (now six) districts of Kumaon was about 50 per cent of this total, and spread over about 7 per cent of the area of Uttar Pradesh. These figures are misleading to a certain extent. The relatively low density of population does not really indicate an abundance of land. In actual fact, a large part of the land mass in these areas is uninhabitable because of high altitudes and inhospitable terrain. A significant part of the area is very poor marginal land, hardly fit for effective cultivation because of the steep slopes and uneven terrain and with hardly any irrigation apart from the monsoon rains. We shall revert to these points later in this chapter.

The northern boundary is the 'Tibetan ridge' at a mean elevation of 5500 metres above sea level. In the east, the Kali river separates Kumaon from Nepal. The region features numerous mountain ranges, valleys and steeply falling slopes. The Himalayan peaks lie to the north, and the foothills of Tarai and Bhabar lie to the south. The heights above sea level range from 180 metres or more along the foothills to a magnificent 7000 metres in the snow-clad peaks in the north. It is important to remember that part of the old Nainital district lies in the plains, generally referred to as Tarai area.

Most of it is in the recently created Udham Singh Nagar
district, which is fertile agricultural land with a number of large
farms. The nature of the geography and the economy in this
area is more akin to the adjoining plains. Our main area of
interest is in the hill areas of Kumaon, though we shall refer
to the plains areas of Kumaon frequently.

The entire region is one of great contrasts and varying
landscapes. The steepness of the slopes as well as the
sharpness of the contours are the most striking feature of
the northern parts. What is even more striking is the contrast
between the variety and diversity of forests, vegetation and
climate in the mountainous terrain, and the comparative
uniformity of the Tarai plains.

The geography and the economy are more closely inter-
related in the hill areas than in the plains. The varying
altitudes and the relative climatic conditions have their own
effects on the possible alternative land-uses, industrial
potential and other economic activity. The nature and extent
of the slopes have their own consequences for cultivation,
water absorption, soil erosion and other aspects important
for agricultural and horticultural activities. These are only
some of the many links between geography and economics
that we shall examine in this book.

There is a close and high degree of mutual dependence
between the environment, resources, population and
development. This four-dimensional relationship is even more
important in the  hill areas. To meet the requirements of
increasing population pressure, technology is harnessed by
man in utilizing the natural resources of land, water, etc.  If
the environmental resources are utilized beyond the carrying
capacity provided by nature, resource development may yield
increased income to the population in the short term, but
can affect the same population adversely in the long run. A
typical example of special relevance to the hill areas is the
increased land area brought under cultivation by reducing
forest cover. While this directly adds to the agricultural income

of the cultivating population in that area, the reduction of forest cover can cause long-term damage in the form of increased soil erosion, reduced water availability, etc.

Mitchell has made a distinction between 'resource development' and 'resource management'.[24] Resource development is the actual use of a resource in order to meet human needs whereas the term 'resource management' is much wider and takes into account long-term aspects as well; it includes resource development and conservation over time and space. The main emphasis in resource management is the minimization of long-term environmental catastrophies while maximizing social welfare over time. O'Riordan puts it well: " Resource management tends to emphasize rationality over emotionalism — ecology over engineering".[29]

Many economic activities relating to agriculture, transport, industry, etc. influence and alter the environment in various ways. Sometimes, as has been happening in Kumaon (as indeed in the rest of the Himalayas), these effects can be profoundly adverse. This will in turn negatively affect the medium- and long-term economic development of the region. Thus the "four-point relationship of population, resources, development and environment, gives rise to a complexity of relationships which both the development planner and resource manager have to take into consideration." [46]

Economic development can be broadly described as the process of improvement in income and the standard of living of the population. It is generally felt that there is a conflict between economic development on the one hand and environmental preservation/ecological balance on the other. The latter are essentially long-run concepts. This conflict is more apparent than real as there is no possibility of long-run economic growth if the environment is not preserved and the ecological balance is upset.

'Sustainable development' is the current buzzword in environmental literature. This really means resource development which takes into account environmental constraints. What are the major environmental constraints in the development process? They are, firstly, the need to preserve exhaustible, depletable resources and, secondly, the need to preserve and maintain the ecological balance. One writer notes that:

> ... the need of the fragile Himalayan mountain region is to devise an environmental resource management system which strikes a balance between the sustainable livelihood needs of the regional population on the one hand, and the imperative of restoring and maintaining the ecological balance on the other.[46]

Our present discussion will centre round the above theme of sustainable economic development. Undoubtedly, efforts have been made to develop the economy of Kumaon by the government as well as private agencies. These efforts have been wide-ranging, from agricultural and horticultural development to the promotion of industries and tourism. However, after all these years, the hill areas of Kumaon are still listed among the more backward regions of the country, with an agricultural sector characterised by low productivity, and an industrial sector which is hardly noticeable. The main income which sustains a majority of the rural areas of Kumaon is partly from tourism and substantially from the 'money-order economy' that is supported by Kumaonis working outside the hill areas, in the defence forces and elsewhere. How has this come about?

### Land-use Pattern in the Kumaon

If we look at agriculture in the Kumaon hills, the scenario is not particularly encouraging. The average holding size is very small, and even that is subdivided and fragmented. Consolidation of holdings, which has been adopted as a regular programme with some degree of success in the rest of the state, especially in the plains, has hardly been attempted in Kumaon. The landholding per capita is around .12 hectare in the Upper Kosi area (a major catchment area of Kumaon), for which the latest figures are available. This would mean a family holding size of about .5 to .6 hectare, which would in most cases be fragmented into three or four subholdings. The pattern in most other parts of the hill areas of Kumaon is more or less the same. The only part of the Kumaon region which has large holdings is in the part of the old Nainital district now known as Udham Singh Nagar district; but this plains area of the former Nainital district is agriculturally a different world altogether, featuring large farms and mechanized cultivation.

The small size of the holdings is not the only factor that militates against an efficient and productive agriculture in the hill areas. The nature of the terrain has also to be considered. S.D. Pant, writing in 1935, describes it thus:

The fields are quite unlike the artificial sub-divisions of the wide, level plains; they resemble rather a gigantic flight of steps, ascending from the banks of the stream towards the summits of the hills. These are known as terraces. An ingenious method of adapting hillsides for cultivation, terracing is the only effective means of checking soil erosion.... Without terracing, agriculture here would be impossible. Terracing requires two simultaneous operations. The mountainside, selected for its form and gradient, is attacked with hoe or pickaxe. The stones, as they are dug and sorted out, are built into a loose retaining wall at the lower edge of the sloping strip. The newly broken soil, consisting chiefly of coarse gravel, is then thrown and dumped against the loosely built stone wall... thus, walls above walls are constructed, roughly parallel to one another, working from the base towards the summit, until the whole slope is terraced.[31]

The initial process of conversion of a whole ridge can take several years. The maintenance of terraces is quite difficult and involves a lot of hard work against the forces of nature such as rain water running down the slopes.

A significant portion of the land area in Kumaon hills, as in the rest of the Himalayas, is not useful either for habitation or cultivation. Areas at a height of more than 4500 metres above sea level are permanently under snow. Cultivated land accounts for less than 30 per cent of the region's geographical area. Nearly 40 per cent of the area is under forests of different types. The largest proportion of agricultural land is to be found between a height of about 750 to 1500 metres above sea level. As much as 70 per cent of the resident population is engaged in cultivation, mainly in the absence of alternative means of livelihood and not because agriculture is profitable to them.

Agriculture, as it is practised in Kumaon, is essentially an uneconomic pursuit at present except in some scattered pockets in relatively fertile and irrigated valley areas in the lower altitudes. Generally, agriculture contributes between 15 to 40 per cent of the household income, and meets only about a third of the annual foodgrain requirements, even in the relatively prosperous areas of Kumaon. There are two types of cultivation, known in Kumaon as *upraun* and *talaun*. *Upraun*, or rain-fed cultivation, is prevalent in the higher elevations and mid-slopes, and is usually without irrigation. Coarse grains such as *mandua*, some varieties of pulses, some paddy and wheat, barley and soyabean are grown here, though the productivity levels are abysmally low. The increasing population pressure, taken together with the limited alternative occupations, has put further pressure on cultivable land as a result of which more and more marginal land in the higher slopes has been brought under the plough. A major paradox observed in Kumaon is that cropping intensity is higher in the mountainous parts than in the more fertile valleys or the highly productive Tarai-Bhabar in the

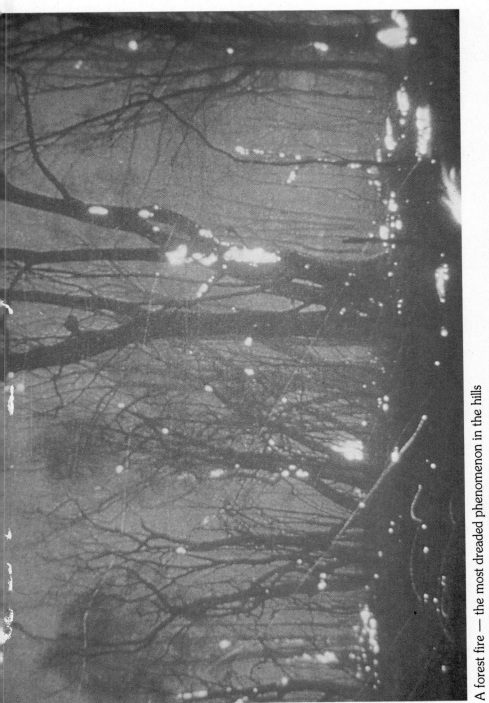

A forest fire — the most dreaded phenomenon in the hills

A river valley broad enough to permit cultivation

Pithoragarh town — located in a rich and fertile valley, which should have been utilised for cultivation

Unscientific mining activity, which is destroying fertile land, and making the hills unstable

plains area of Rudrapur. The cropping intensity in some of these areas is 150 per cent to 170 per cent in some tracts, but the productivity is indeed very low. Except for Nainital district (which includes large areas in the plains recently converted into the separate district of Udham Singh Nagar), production of foodgrains has remained static or declined during recent years in the other districts of Kumaon, i.e. in the hill areas.

Apart from *upraun* (rain-fed cultivation), which occupies more than 80 per cent of the cultivated area in most parts of Kumaon, there is *talaun* cultivation which is characterised by fine and deep soil cover, moderate temperatures, gentle slopes in the lower altitudes and reasonably regular irrigation water supply. Paddy and pulses are grown here during the *kharif* season, and wheat, barley, mustard and potatoes during *rabi*. Potato is more like a commercial crop in many areas and yields good income to the cultivators. Hill potato farming has a very favourable feature, viz. that it is available at a time when the potato season in the plains is over. Apart from this, the hill potato is generally regarded as more tasty and commands a premium in the market.

The problem of soil erosion has already been mentioned. Its implications for hill agriculture are enormous. In recent years, the erosion of top soils in the Kumaon hills, as indeed in the rest of the Himalayas, has increased at a truly alarming rate. The increase in soil erosion is substantially due to man-made causes. The erosion of top soils reduces the fertility of the hill farmlands and increases surface run-off of water, and thus adversely affects many economic activities in the hills. It also increases sedimentation and siltation in the plains. The riverbeds in the major rivers in the plains have also risen because of the increasing siltation. Some experts have estimated that nearly 20 per cent of the live storage capacity of our medium and major dams have already been silted up, which would mean a loss of irrigation potential of more than 60,000 hectares every year. Sedimentation at the rate of nearly three times more than what was initially estimated has not only reduced the amount of irrigation potential of these projects, but also reduced their life. Increased sedimentation and siltation have undoubtedly major implications for agriculture in the hill areas.

## Deforestation and Loss of Vegetal Cover

While the average surface run-off of water in most parts of the region is around 18 per cent for cultivated land, it is less than 1 per cent in the forest area. This obviously means that almost all the water falling on or flowing into the forest area enriches the water resources of the soil. We have discussed the water resources in Kumaon in greater detail in Chapter V. Here we are concerned mainly with the relevance of the state of water absorption and run-off on hill agriculture.

It is well known that the surface run-off of water increases with decreasing vegetation and forests in any area, and the Kumaon hills are no exception. Large-scale denudation and destruction of forest cover have resulted in reduced availability of water and energy for agricultural and horticultural activities. Road construction activities also have caused damage to the mountains by reducing vegetation and increasing the movement of debris down the slopes, thus increasing sedimentation in the hill streams, increased soil erosion and reduced soil fertility. Sediment output in many parts of Kumaon has increased from 70 kg. per hectare in 1980 to 90 kg. per hectare in 1990, i.e. by nearly 30 per cent in a short span of ten years.

The number of grazing cattle has also overtaken the capacity of the existing forests and pastures. One author has estimated that, as against an optimum 15 acres of land required per head of cattle, the actual land available in the Kumaon is only about 1 to 1.5 acres. Increased grazing pressure has also contributed to deforestation by lopping for fodder and destruction of vegetation on the slopes by cattle movements.

In this depressing scenario of increased soil erosion, reduced water availability and soil fertility, and depleted forest cover, the increasing population pressure has added further problems .

Madhav Ashish, an observer of the Kumaon scene for nearly fifty years till his death in 1997, has written perceptively about the problems of the UP hills. What he wrote in 1978 is worth quoting in detail. Madhav Ashish writes:

> ... every acre of hill cultivation ... requires at least ten times the amount in terms of pasture and forest. With the increase of population and consequent extension of cultivation, the minimum proportion of one of cultivation to ten of pasture ... has been lost. The drain on pasture and forest is therefore greater than the rate of natural regeneration. ... The environmental capital (grass, fodder, forest) is being used up faster than it replaces itself. Furthermore, natural regeneration of felled forest is checked by grazing and trampling. Therefore, hill agriculture is dooming itself. Population growth has brought families to the point where, with few exceptions, they obtain a meagre three months' food from their fields. All working age men are in non-agricultural employment, but they leave their families with cows and buffaloes in the hills. There is therefore little or no abject poverty because they all have cash from the plains to purchase plains-grown grain. All the families keep cattle and rape the pastures and forests. Suggested answer: stop all cultivation (with the possible exception of fertile river valleys) and rehabilitate the population into a forest-based economy.[4]

Madhav Ashish estimated more than twenty years ago that total environmental collapse of the Kumaon was less than one hundred years away if the current practices continued.

Viewed from this perspective, it is only the 'money order economy' which sustains the hills. Many of the young and middle-aged men have migrated to the plains in search of employment. The defence forces, the paramilitary forces such as the Border Security Force, domestic employment in cities, etc. — none of these employment avenues have been left unexplored by the Kumaoni in his ceaseless quest for gainful livelihood outside the hill areas.

The migration to the plains is an ongoing movement. The contribution to the hill areas by such migrants, who send a substantial part of their earnings home,cannot be underestimated. There are quite a few persons who have migrated with their entire families to the plains, but a very large number are those who have left their families behind in their hill villages. A *jawan* in the Indian Army earns upwards of thirty to forty thousand rupees a year, even a fraction of which cannot be earned by him in his farming activity on the limited and mostly unirrigated land available to his family. However, the sociological implications of the 'money order economy' cannot be overlooked. In many villages, a good percentage of the able-bodied males would be earning their livelihood in the plains, visiting their homes during periods of leave. Of course, these men would return to live in their hill homes after retirement from a lifetime of employment outside the Kumaon. In most cases, the women and children stay in the hills, looking after the land and the cattle they possess. In the foreseeable future there seems no ready alternative to this state of affairs. In fact, the money order economy may well have saved many families in the hill areas from destitution.

One asset of the Kumaoni is that he has proved to be very capable and efficient as part of a disciplined force, such as the defence or paramilitary forces. Nowhere is this more evident than in the success of the Kumaoni soldiers and officers in the Indian Army. Along with the Garhwalis, their exploits during the wars on India's borders during the last fifty years have brought them considerable fame as dependable and heroic soldiers. Most families in the Kumaon hills have one or more male members employed in the Army or paramilitary forces such as the Border Security Force.

The armed forces are thus a very important part of life in the Kumaon hills. Not only do they provide a respectable livelihood and relatively good income to many Kumaonis, it also implies that after their retirement (which can be in their late forties or early fifties) these disciplined, fit and hardworking men return to the villages, and possibly can be the focal point of many development programmes.

In view of the important role played by the Army in Kumaoni life, we are devoting a separate chapter to the history of the Kumaon regiment.

Paradoxically, it is the income earned from the defence forces and other jobs in the plains that often pays for further extending the uneconomic terrace cultivation in Kumaon, increasing deforestation and siltation, reducing the water availability in the mountain springs and streams, and adding to the degradation of the environment of the region. The money earned outside the hill areas not only buys more than half the foodgrains consumed in the hill areas but is also used to extend hill agriculture for short-term benefits and long-term damage to the environment.

A drastic solution to the problem is to progressively phase out hill agriculture as it is practised at present, except in the fertile valley areas of the Kumaon hills, and a large part of the present cultivated land reforested or planted with fruit trees if Kumaon is to survive. The hill areas cannot maintain as many cattle as they are doing at present for the reasons we have discussed earlier. The income of the population perhaps will basically come from four sources: firstly, from forest-based activities; secondly, from small industries in and around the inhabited areas, partly based on timber and horticulture; thirdly, from tourism; and fourthly, from the 'money order' economy. Madhav Ashish visualizes it thus:

> Looking forward fifty years in imagination, I can see the springs with greater and more continuous flow, the river waters clear as crystal. Men move among the pine trees, tapping resin, and the crash of a falling tree tells where more men are felling selected timber. The roar of transport comes from forest service roads, and the whine of a sawmill rises from the valley. Smoke rises from a turpentine factory and the gleam of dam water shows where a hydrogenerator makes power for the mill and lights up the villages. And on the ridges, facing the unparalleled Himalayan snows, stand tourist hotels. Parties of hikers trudge the footpaths, hoping to see *kakar* or sambar, and fearing to meet leopard and bear.[4]

If the hills get more and more denuded, there is less water absorption, and silting and flooding of the plains will increase progressively. As hill agriculture is not viable, except in a few fertile valleys, the fact its extension reduces forest cover and because cattle grazing on the current scale cannot be sustained for long, the gradual phasing out of these activities and moving towards an economy based on forests, small industries and tourism appears to be the only viable solution to the Kumaon problem. The practical implementation of such a solution is, of course, an entirely different matter.

This inevitably leads us to the mundane but pertinent question — what are the likely income-generating activities for the hill population in the future? We have already seen the significance of the 'money order economy' for the hill areas. In the Kumaon region, a very large number of families owe their main source of income to the earnings outside the hills of Kumaonis who have migrated to areas in the plains to earn their livelihood. The defence and paramilitary forces have attracted a substantial segment of these migrants.

In addition to the contribution of the 'money order economy', what are the likely internal income-generating activities? This question becomes even more important in the context of the new state of Uttaranchal, which incorporates the Kumaon and Garhwal regions of Uttar Pradesh.

We shall discuss these possibilities under four heads, viz. industries, horticulture, tourism and power projects.

Writing in 1935, S.D. Pant had listed out a few small industries such as basket-weaving (using a local variety of bamboo called *ringal* as raw material), and shawl and carpet weaving as the main possibilities in the industrial sector in the Kumaon region.[31] It is noteworthy that even today, except for such small-scale industrial efforts, there is still very little industrial development in the Kumaon hills.

The hill districts have virtually no industries of any significance or size. In a recent published estimate, less than 3 per cent of the labour employed in factories in UP came from Kumaon and Garhwal. If we exclude the plains areas and consider only the hill portion of these districts, this figure comes down to just .2 per cent, showing a very negligible level of industrialization, compared even to the remaining parts of UP. We must remember that UP itself is industrially and agriculturally quite backward in comparison to most other states in India.

It is true that manufacturing industry on a factory scale is unlikely to develop to a significant extent in the hill areas for various reasons. Mainly because of difficult terrain, associated transport costs and limited availability of local raw materials (except for forest-based and horticultural products), establishment of most manufacturing industries, may prove to be non-viable in the hill areas. Often, it has been talked about in general terms about 'electronic' industries being suitable for the non-polluted atmosphere of the hills.

However, it has been found from experience all over the world as well as in India that electronics-based industries are more easily established and are more viable in areas where there is a considerable amount of highly skilled personnel available, supported by the facilities and infrastructure of reasonably large cities. Further, modern air conditioning effectively eliminates the pollution as far as the production facilities in the factory are concerned, and the other advantages of highly skilled personnel, supporting infrastructure and the attractions/facilities of city life generally make the costs of air conditioning worthwhile from the industry's point of view in most cases.

It appears, therefore, that industrial activity in Kumaon hills may remain confined to a few scattered small-scale units producing fruit juices and jams, some others making hand-woven carpets and shawls. Perhaps there will be also some scope for some furniture-making and forest-based units, but the increasing restrictions on felling of trees and use of forest produce make this a very limited option. Any industrial unit has to be based on availability of local raw materials or skills, or on specific locational advantages. On all these points, the Kumaon hill region presents very limited scope for industrial activity.

Industrialization, in the normally accepted sense of the term, is therefore not likely to be the solution to Kumaon's problems even in the long run. We have to look for other means of income-generation for the Kumaonis.

We had earlier dwelt on the limitations and problems of hill agriculture. Horticulture, i.e. the cultivation of fruits and vegetables, has considerable potential in the hill areas, which are specially suitable for growing temperate fruits such as apples, apricots, plums, peaches, etc. at altitudes between 5000 to 7000 feet above sea level. There are, however, some problems here. The average size of land holding is, as we have noticed earlier, very small, being about 1 hectare per capita. In most cases, even this holding is not held in one contiguous piece, but is separated into several smaller plots not adjacent to one another — which is known as 'subdivision and fragmentation' of agricultural holdings. The small size and the fragmented nature of land holdings also militate against the development of efficient fruit cultivation. Marketing is also a problem to the owner of only a few fruit trees. In such cases, the organization of transport and marketing is inevitably left to the middleman, who pockets a major part of the income from horticulture. The small cultivator has no holding capacity for any reasonable length of time and has to sell his produce to the middleman immediately after the fruits are ready for plucking. In theory, fruit cooperatives are an answer to this problem. Realistically, it appears unlikely that they can be organized on a significant scale to make an impact.

These are some of the reasons why horticulture has not made much progress in the Kumaon and Garhwal regions. However, we must remember that Himachal Pradesh, where climatic and other conditions are largely similar, has made substantial progress in the cultivation and marketing of temperate fruits, especially apples. The marketing and transport infrastructure in Himachal have been developed mostly by private initiative with government support.

Horticulture must, therefore, be regarded as an area where there is still scope for development and growth in Kumaon. Apart from the cultivation of temperate fruits, the cultivation and marketing of vegetables also presents a good opportunity for income generation. We have seen a upsurge in this regard in the many valleys of the Kumaon in recent years — especially in regard to vegetables such as tomatoes, capsicum, cauliflower, etc. for the cultivation of which the hill areas have some advantages. There is another reason which makes vegetable cultivation profitable — many of these vegetables grow in the hills in those months of the year when they are 'off-season' in the plains. With the development of road transport and the improvement in road communications, vegetable cultivation is bound to further add to the incomes of the Kumaon villages in the coming years.

## Tourism

Kumaon has some of the most scenically beautiful places in the world. The scenic beauty and the climate are the main characteristics of the hill areas which attract the discerning as well as the casual tourist. The hills present different types of attractions in different seasons for tourists of all age-groups and backgrounds. What we should aim at developing, is ecologically sustainable tourism, i.e. tourism which does not add to environmental degradation of the type we have discussed in an earlier chapter. Already an adequate network of roads exists in these hills to enable the tourists to reach many earlier inaccessible areas. There have been considerable improvements in the accommodation facilities available in many of the resorts and towns. There are also opportunities for trekking for the younger tourists, while the older tourists can take in the mountain views and enjoy the clean mountain air. In a later chapter, the tourist opportunities have been described.

Whenever a tourist spends any money during his visit — e.g. on hiring a local taxi, staying in a hotel or buying things from the local shops as souvenirs or for his daily needs during his stay — it adds directly or indirectly to the incomes in the hill areas. Of course, it is a challenge for the hill administration to attract the tourists to these areas while, at the same times, preserving and protecting the hill environment

Chapter 4

# Gods and Goddesses of Kumaon

In Kumaon, as elsewhere in India, the predominant religion is Hinduism, but when the temple bells ring out here, it is not only for the traditional gods of the Hindu pantheon — Shiva, Vishnu and Shakti — but also for a host of other gods and demons, who have a very strong hold on the local imagination. In the very early period of Kumaoni history, the population, whether original inhabitants of the region or immigrants from other parts of India or outside, were forced to eke out a rough existence in a hostile environment. Inevitably, the elements that frightened them and needed to be propitiated became their gods. We do not really know what were the earliest objects of worship, but at some point there came a stage when they began to believe in superhuman spirits who were known as 'demons' and had to be propitiated. Local legend and mythology, and even historical characters, also provided them with gods. Interestingly enough, the *pahari* still worships these gods and demons and even in temples erected to Shiva, Vishnu or the mother goddess Shakti, the 'old' gods often have an honourable place. Incidentally, it must be pointed out that this is an all-India phenomenon, and though attempts are always being made to Sanskritize religion and bring it within the bounds of conservatism, rural India still continues to maintain a special place for its localized gods and spirits. They have either slipped into the traditional pantheon or maintained a separate identity,. but they have managed to coexist peacefully. The anthropologist S.C. Dube, defines the religion of the Hindus thus:

> A text-book knowledge of the religious lore of India and an acquaintance with her ancient classics and their modern expositions will hardly give us a true picture of the actual religious beliefs, thoughts, feelings and practices of the people now living in the countryside. A classification of their religious beliefs and rituals is not an easy task. Folklore and myths, religious teachings of saint-poets, and contacts with persons having knowledge of scriptures and popular religious books have all influenced their ideology. Consequently their religion is a mixture of animism, animalism and polytheism with the occasional appearance of monotheism also. To these must be added a living faith in spirits, ghosts, demons, witches and magic.[6]

To this worship of ghosts, spirits and demons, the term 'animism' is generally applied. The word really means the worship of spirits which could be either good or bad, but which are extremely powerful. They must be propitiated, and either persuaded to protect the worshipper, or dissuaded from harming him. Efforts of reformers or spiritual leaders from the plains, all directed at Sanskritizing the religious beliefs and customs of the *paharis* and generally bringing them in line with the orthodox religion prevailing in the plains, have made them sensitive about their original (and preferred) religious practices and, as a result, they will not discuss them with outsiders unless they are found to be sympathetic and uncensorious.

The mother goddess or Shakti is the most important deity in this area, and ancient mythology credits her with having created not only the world but also the three gods of the traditional Hindu pantheon, Shiva, Vishnu and Brahma. She is worshipped in several aspects all over Kumaon and Garhwal, and many local legends are centred round the goddess, the most popular incarnation being that of Nanda Devi. She is now linked with Naina Devi, but originally, Nanda Devi was identified with Parvati, the consort of Shiva, and Naina Devi was a borrowing from the Greek goddess Nana, who came into the Himalayas with the Indo-Greeks and Kushan kings. The temptation to trace these links between Kumaoni myth and mainstream Hindu legend (or, in fact, any other school of mythology) must be resisted as the stories clash in many areas. Scholars feel that this is the result of trying to incorporate the pre-Aryan deities who presided over these regions into the regular Hindu pantheon of gods and goddesses.

The Naina Devi legend as it exists in the Kumaon, runs thus. Her father, Dakshaprajapati, organised a great sacrifice, but he refused to invite her consort, Shiva, as he disapproved of his lifestyle and appearance. Daksha is supposed to have described him thus:

> He roams about in dreadful cemeteries, attended by hosts of goblins and spirits, like a madman, naked, with dishevelled hair, laughing, weeping and bathed in the ashes of funeral pyres, wearing a garland of skulls and ornaments of human bones, insane, beloved by the insane, the lord of beings whose nature is essentially darkness.

Undeterred, Naina went to her father's house for the ceremony, accompanied by her husband, but they were grossly insulted and turned away at the gate by Dakshaprajapati. Distraught, Naina committed suicide. A grief-stricken Shiva picked up her body, and danced with her all over the world. As he was carrying her away, her eyes fell out near the temple of Pashan Devi in Nainital. The

temple that now stands near the Nainital lake is the temple
of Naina Devi and she has given her name to the famous
hill-station.

Nanda Devi is supposed to be the Kumaoni incarnartion
of Parvati, the wife of Lord Shiva. The local legend says that
Nanda and Sunanda were both daughters of a local chieftain.
One day they were attacked by a mad buffalo, and though
they hid in a banana plantation, they were both killed. Nanda
Devi, the highest mountain in the Indian Himalayas is now
her abode. The feast of this goddess, which is very important
in both Kumaon and Garhwal, is celebrated annually in the
month of August. It was believed that the buffalo sacrifice
that used to mark the occasion originated because Nanda
requested people to give her a buffalo every year as one of
the species had killed her. The songs and *jagars* (a special
type of religious chanting) that mark the festival actually relate
to the story that Nanda Devi descends every year from the
ice-cold mountain top where her husband Shiva has his
home, and comes to her mother's house for a brief vacation.
On the day of the festival she is sent back to his abode with
all due fanfare, and with a plenitude of gifts.

The annual Nanda Devi fair is celebrated with great pomp
in Almora. The buffalo sacrifice has been replaced with the
offering of coconuts, but the event is still impressive. While
the priests chant the required *mantras* round a sacred fire,
the young men dance desultorily to the beat of a copper
drum. But the leisurely pace of events is maintained only till
the *jagar* begins. The male oracle on whom the spirit of
Nanda Devi descends, arrives on the shoulders of one of his
companions and begins by settling problems of the villagers
on behalf of the Devi. Soon, the climax of the ceremony is
reached. Bill Aitken in his book *The Nanda Devi Affair*
describes it thus:

The Shilpkar drummer emerges from the shadows of the
bonfire and suddenly assumes a presiding presence. His

small drum emits the most electrifying coda and one feels the hair bristle as 'forces from the other side are challenged to appear in answer to these compulsive sorcerers' drum beats. Hissing, slavering and ranting, the possessed *shaman* is borne into the ring of fire. Pop-eyed with the vacancy of a soul dislodged, he shivers violently and has to be forcibly restrained from leaping off the shoulders of his bearers. Between his teeth is clenched the Devi's dagger to symbolise that the mouthpiece of the goddess will brook no obstacle.[1]

As the drumming reaches its crescendo, the dancing intensifies. The dancers themselves seem possessed, and in the midst of grotesque shadows thrown up by the flames, mothers hold up their children to be blessed by the Goddess.

Every twelve years (give or take a few years), a great *yatra* sets out to the foot of the Nanda Devi mountain. A four-horned goat, which is provided by the villagers of Nauti in Garhwal — who incidentally organise not only the great pilgrimage but also the much smaller annual ones — is taken to a spot near the base of the mountain. When the pilgrims reach their destination, it is covered with garlands and sent off up the mountain trail. Legend has it that it runs straight up the mountain unhesitatingly. Bill Aitken's book describes one such *yatra*, the route it took and the rituals involved during the pilgrimage, which incidentally took place 19 years after the previous one.

The pilgrimages to Nanda Devi have been linked by anthropologists to a ritualized re-enactment of the *pahari* bride's (in this case, Nanda Devi's) return to her *sauryas* (her in-laws' home) from her *mait* (mother's house). All married women identify themselves with the event and, though they do not go on the pilgrimage, the songs sung at the villages the Devi's procession traverses reflect the poignancy of the occasion.

The one given below is a translation of one of the songs
sung during the Nanda Devi *yatra*, quoted by William Sax.[41]

Victory to Nanda, Amba, and Jagdamba!
Victory to Nanda and Jagdamba Bhavani!
Victory to the Great Goddess, Bearer of the Parasol,
Victory to the Mother of the World!

May the sixty-four Nandas, the daughters of Daksa, the
Lord of Creatures,
Sisters of the Royal Sages be generous!
In Nauti, Almora, Siroli and Pratyeka,
May the daughter of the gods be successful, Victory....

I will serve you by singing this song,
I will make offerings to your feet,
I will sacrifice buffaloes in your place,
Success will come to our village, Victory....

And so the song goes on, each verse reflecting the sadness
of a young girl leaving her care-free girlhood behind and
going back to the responsibilities of her married home.

The most famous of the temples to Nanda Devi is the
one in Almora. The British Commissioner of Kumaon, Traill,
tried to shift the temple to a spot which he considered more
convenient from the point of view of establishing a new
township. A short while later, while on a trip to the Pindari
glacier, he was struck by snow blindness and his advisors
convinced him that this was an indication of the goddess'
displeasure. He moved the temple back to its original site,
and his sight was miraculously restored.

Another dominant deity of the Himalayas is Shiva whose
abode has always Mount Kailash, but who seems to have
evolved through the ages, accruing to himself the qualities
of other local deities of Kumaon and Garhwal in becoming
the figure he is today. Some early sculptures show figures

A landslide on Almora-Pithoragarh road

Terrace cultivation is the normal method of growing crops in Kumaon

Mixed forest of oak, rhododendron, horsechestnut and pine in the Kumaon region

Rufous turtle doves

which seem to be of Pasupati, who perhaps merged later with Agni and Rudra to become the Shiva of Kedarnath.

Many archaelogists feel that the Pasupati images were really early Buddhist or Jain icons. These artifacts are few in number and not easily identifiable, but it is believed that Buddhism was well established in Kumaon by the seventh century AD. The decline of Buddhism set in soon after, an event locally attributed to the arrival upon the scene of the Adi Shankaracharya, (788 — 820 AD) who is supposed to have visited Jageshwar and Gangolihat in Kumaon before moving on to Garhwal where he established the two large temples of Kedarnath and Badrinath.

Atkinson is of the view that the form of Buddhism prevailing in this region was also suffering from the ailments that assailed Brahmanism at this period — a decadence associated with Tantric practices — and Shankaracharya, in his great reformist zeal, eliminated the one and cleansed the other. In order to revive orthodox Hinduism in Kumaon and Nepal, Shankaracharya began by dispersing the Buddhist monks and nuns. He then established the worship of Siva at Kedarnath and of Vishnu at Badrinath. In place of the old Baudhmargi priests, who were disbanded, came priests from Kerala who manage these two temples even today. Pilgrimage to the two shrines was encouraged as the constant influx of pilgrims ensured that the area did not relapse into Buddhism again. In all fairness, it must be admitted that there seems to be no historical evidence that Adi Shankaracharya visited these regions, but popular belief attributes the establishment of the Kedarnath-Badrinath temples to him.

The maximum number of temples in the Kumaon are those dedicated to Shiva. Then come the temples of Devi or Shakti. Vishnu temples are comparatively few in number, and those dedicated to Rama and Krishna are modern in origin. Shiva is very obviously the god of the mountains, as his abode is on Kailash. Early texts described Rudra as the father of the *maruts* or the winds, or equated him with Agni, the god of fire, but later the two personae seem to have merged. Professor Whitney, as quoted by E.T. Atkinson, says that the Kumaon Himalaya is responsible for the evolution of modern Saivism:

> The introduction of an entirely new divinity from the mountains of the north has been supposed, who was grafted in upon the ancient religion by being identified with Rudra, or again a blending of some of Agni's attributes with those of Rudra to originate a new development. Perhaps neither of these may be necessary: Shiva may be a local form of Rudra, arisen under the influences of peculiar climatic relations in the districts from which he made his way down into Hindustan proper....[5]

The most important, as well as the most beautiful, Shiva temple in Kumaon is that of Jageshwar, 35 km. from Almora. This is a temple complex consisting of 108 temples built over a period of five centuries. Most of these temples are small, but there are a few large ones as well. Magnificent *deodar* forests surround the complexes of Jageshwar and Dandeshwar (half a kilometre apart), thereby making them aesthetically as well as spiritually satisfying. The oldest temple at Jageshwar is the one built to Mrityunjaya, and it dates from the eighth century AD, i.e. the early part of the Katyuri period. The most important, however, is the one which houses the Jyotirlinga, one of the twelve all over India.

The old story associated with the establishment of the Jyotirlingas, runs thus. There are several versions of the legend, but the broad outlines are similar. This is the one current at Jageshwar, which is the Jyotirling associated with *Darukavan* in the ancient Sanskrit sloka.

सौराष्ट्रे सोमनाथं च श्रीशैले मल्लिकार्जुनम्। उज्जयिन्यां महाकालमोंकारे परमेश्वरम्॥
केदारं हिमवत्पृष्ठे डाकिन्यां भीमशंकरम्। वाराणस्यां च विश्वेशं त्र्यम्बकं गौतमीतटे॥
वैद्यनाथं चिताभूमौ नागेशं दारुकावने। सेतुबन्धे च रामेशं घुशमेशं तु शिवालये॥

This sloka details the various places where the *Jyotirlingas* have appeared and where they are now worshipped.

The temples are those of: 1. Somnath (Saurashtra in Gujarat), 2. Mallikarjun in Srisailam (Andhra Pradesh), 3. Mahakaleshwar on the banks of the Shipra in Ujjain (Madhya Pradesh), 4. Onkareshwar on the banks of the Narmada river in Malwa (Madhya Pradesh), 5. Kedarnath in Garhwal (Uttaranchal), 6. Bhimshankar near Ahmednagar (the old name of the hill where the temple is situated was Dakini in Maharashtra), 7. Vishwanath in Varanasi (Uttaranchal), 8. Trimbakeshwar near Nasik on the banks of the Godavari (Maharashtra), 9. Vaidyanath in the Samthal region (Orissa), 10. Jageshwar near Almora (Uttaranchal), 11. Rameshwaram (Tamil Nadu) and 12. Ghushmeshwar (or Ghrushmeshwar) near Veruk, the original name of the village where the Ellora caves are found (Maharashtra).

After Shiva and Parvati were insulted by King Daksha, Parvati immolated herself and became *sati*. In his deep distress, Shiva raged over the whole world, carrying her body in his arms. Later, appalled by the destruction he had caused, he settled down to perform penance at Vriddha Jageshwar, above Jageshwar. One day, the wives of the seven sages, (*saptarishis*) saw him while they were cutting grass and, struck with wonder at the beauty and majesty of this unknown *rishi*, they fell unconscious. When they did not come home in the evening, their husbands came looking for them. Shiva was still meditating, and had no idea of what was happening around him, but the sages cursed him, holding him responsible for their wives' dereliction of duty. Shiva suffered the punishment they inflicted upon him, and a great darkness fell upon the world, till Vishnu gathered up the darkness and dispersed it in the shape of the twelve *Jyotirlingas*, which are pilgrimage spots all over the country.

Another local legend says that when the original temple at Jageshwar was being constructed, a demon living in

Vriddha Jageshwar made it a practice to come down every night and destroy whatever had been built during the day. The architect then had a brilliant idea. He got his men to provide the demon with mountains of meat every evening so that the demon was so busy eating it at night that he had no time to meddle with the temples. During the Rohilla invasion of Kumaon (1743), Jageshwar, already a very rich temple, was the only one in the area to escape being pillaged. Its salvation is attributed to swarms of bees that attacked the marauding armies and drove them away.

Folk gods of varied origin have also been added to the traditional Hindu pantheon. Some of these, as has been mentioned earlier, have descended from pre-Aryan animism and demonism, others from local legends associated with princely families or regional heroes. These are usually divided into various categories, i.e. those of *kul devtas* (family gods), *gram devtas* (village gods), *naga devtas* (snake gods), *bhumi devtas* (land gods) and *veers* (heroes). Harju, for example, is the name of a local village god who dominates in a group of villages near where the authors live in Ranikhet. Priests from Hardwar come once every few years (it is supposed to be every seven years, but the schedule does not work out with great regularity), to conduct a series of all-night *jagars*, and sacrifices. The animals for the sacrifice — goats or chickens — are provided by householders. The *puja* lasts for twenty-one days and, on the final day, a grand sacrifice of a goat, a pig and a chicken is performed. Significantly enough, the flesh is not eaten. It is buried on the outskirts of the village, which leads us to believe that this is one of the *gram devtas* whose job it is to protect the village. In addition to these gods, there are also ghosts and fairies who have to be propitiated on various occasions in order to prevent them from harassing human beings.

Goril, or Golu *devta*, however, belongs exclusively to Kumaon and has no equivalent anywhere else. He is the Kumaoni god of justice. The best known Golu temple is the one at Chitai near Almora, which is always thronged by supplicants and grateful devotees. Many of them sacrifice goats in gratitude for favours received, or in anticipation of boons to be granted. Thousands of bells donated by devotees hang from the ceiling and along the approach to the temple. There are also thousands of dust-laden documents dangling from the ceiling — copies of legal petitions to Golu *devta* asking for his intercession in personal disputes. In fact, on a recent visit, we found a copy of a supplicant's application form for recruitment into the Kumaon regiment with a small personal note to Golu asking him to ensure his success in the recruitment tests. There are three major temples in the Kumaon devoted to Golu, of which Chitai is the most famous. The other two are in Champawat and Ghorakhal, but a large number of small village temples have now reserved a niche for the idol of Golu.

The story of Golu stressing, as it does, the theme of justice has a legendary charm. It runs thus. Once upon a time, Jhalrai, a Katyuri king, went hunting. When he reached a village called Dubachaur, he saw two buffaloes fighting. He tried to separate them, but in vain, and then, as he was very hungry and tired, he sent his servants to look for some water. A servant found his way to a waterfall, but while trying to fill up the pot he was carrying, he splashed some on a beautiful maiden who was meditating nearby. Disturbed, she exclaimed angrily, "Obviously, the servants of a man who cannot even stop buffaloes fighting will be equally incompetent in everything else." Astonished at her omniscience, the servants begged her to accompany them. She did so, and easily separated the two buffaloes, which were still fighting. The king was very impressed with her. He enquired into her background, and found that her name was Kali, and she and her uncle, another local raja, had been engaged in austerities to propitiate one of the deities. She had been disturbed by his servants. The king went with her to meet her uncle, whom he found to be a leper. But Jhalrai was so struck by Kali that he was determined to marry her. After he had served her uncle for some time, the uncle commanded Kali to marry the king. Kali did so, and soon became his favourite queen. Soon she became pregnant, but when the baby was due, the king had to be away from his capital. The other queens were very jealous of Kali, and so, when her son was born, they blindfolded her, took the child away, and substituted a pumpkin for him. Then they put the baby in a cage full of salt, and flung it into the river. The salt turned into sugar, and the baby was nourished on it till the cage was found by a childless fisherman, who decided that it was a gift from the gods, and took it home and raised it as his own. He was named Golu or Goril because the river from which he was rescued was the Gori Ganga.

A few years later, when the boy had grown up a bit, he went to the river bank, taking with him his wooden horse. He made his way to the spot where the queens were washing clothes, and asked them to move out of the way as his horse wanted to drink water. They laughed at him and said, "Can a wooden horse drink water?" Golu replied, "If a queen can give birth to a purnpkin, a wooden horse can certainly drink water." This story was conveyed to the king, who immediately sent for the boy. Golu recounted in court the wrongs that had been inflicted on him and his mother. The king immediately recognised him as his heir apparent, brought the mother back to court (she had been banished) and punished the wicked queens. In due course, Golu succeeded his father, and ruled for many years, revered by all for his fairness and impartiality. He seems to have become an object of worship even in his lifetime.

Bholanath is another very popular folk god. He and his consort Barhini have now been identified with Mahadev and his consort, and have therefore entered the orthodox Hindu pantheon, but Bholanath's origins are really in folk mythology, and form one of the connecting links between the orthodox school of Hinduism and the world of ghosts and goblins that is common to all mountainous countries. He was reputed to be the elder son of King Udai Chand of Almora, who took to evil ways, and was exiled. The younger son succeeded his father on the throne as Gyan Chand and was very popular, but after some years, Bholanath re-entered Almora in disguise. The news was communicated to the king, who ordered that he be killed. After his death he became a *bhut* or ghost, as did his wife Barhini and their unborn child. As they began to harass the villagers, they had to be propitiated. Many temples have been erected to them, where worship is regular and frequent. Soon after the British conquest of Almora, the ensuing confusion in the administration resulted in these temples falling into disuse, "but Bholanath showered such storms of stones on the British camp that the English gentlemen at once awoke to the importance of this deity and provided for his worship in a suitable manner".[5] There are eight temples dedicated to Bholanath or Bhairav in Almora. Sometimes, a small iron trident is placed in a corner of a house as an emblem of Bholanath, and is worshipped when the family is in any kind of distress.

Similarly, Gangnath, son of a Nepalese king fell out with his family and became a mendicant. He fell in love with a Brahmin woman and, as a result, was murdered at the instigation of either her husband or her brother (legend is vague at this point). He began to 'harm' people and so rites were evolved to propitiate him and his lady love, Bhana. Gangnath temples are found all over Kumaon. He harasses the young and the beautiful if they do not propitiate him. If anyone is troubled by wicked or powerful people, he prays to Gangnath, who invariably comes to his assistance. Sometimes Gangnath possesses a follower, and through him conveys to the world at large that anyone who gives him the following articles can achieve his heart's desire: to Gangnath himself, a kid, cakes, sweets, beads, a bag and a pair of earrings; for Bhana his mistress, a petticoat, a *dupatta* and

a nose ring; to the child that was killed with them, a coat
and anklets.

Airy is a sylvan god of repellent aspect. He has eyes
on top of his head, and four arms filled with weapons. His
chief attendants, Sau and Bhau, ride on dogs and always
travel with a pack of hunting dogs with bells around their
necks. They are also usually accompanied by hordes of fairies
and goblins, all of whom have their feet turned back to front
to distinguish them from ordinary mortals. Whoever hears
the  bells tinkling round the necks of the dogs is certain to
meet with some calamity. Airy's temples are found in desolate
areas and lonely hilltops.

Chaumu is worshipped in the Jhulaghat Pancheshwar
area. The story goes that once a traveller proceeded to
Champawat carrying in his turban a crystal Shiva linga. At
one point, he wanted to drink water, so he put it down on
the ground. Later, he found that he could not pick it up again
because it had become so heavy. A temple was built on the
spot, and it became a place of pilgrimage. There is a touch
of pastoral simplicity about the cult of Chaumu. He presides
over cattle and, on all Hindu festivals, lamps are lighted and
sweetmeats offered to him. People who have lost their cattle
pray to him to help in their recovery.

Haru and Saim are guardians of the village. Their temples
are usually together, and prolonged *jagars* are conducted in
order to request them to guard the boundaries of the village.
Haru is a beneficent spirit who was, once upon a time, Raja
Harishchand of Champawat. When he became old, he
abdicated and went away to Haridwar, where he took *sanyas*,
and gave himself up to austerity and good works. Saim was
also one of his followers. When they died, they became good
spirits. Kshetrapal too is the tutelary god of fields and
boundaries. He is gentle and beneficent and harasses no one,
but when a new crop is sown, a handful of seed is offered
to him first to protect it from disease or blight. There is a

temple dedicated to him at Jageshwar because he is the guardian spirit of this area.

Kail Bisht, a gentle flute-playing folk god, has a temple dedicated to him at Binsar. Kumaoni drama troupes frequently dramatise the story of Kail Bisht, which has considerable local appeal. His story says that he was a cowherd. The official priest of the King of Almora, Srikrishna Pande, became very grateful to Kail for protecting him from the sorcery of one of his enemies, Naulakhia Pande. Kail achieved this by defeating the demon sent by Naulakhia Pande who was haunting Srikrishna Pande and buried him under a huge rock. But Naulakhia, undeterred, continued his machinations to the extent that he created a wedge between Srikrishna Pande and Kail. Srikrishna asked the king of Almora to have Kail executed, but the king refused to oblige him for he saw the impression of a trident (*trisul*) on Kail's forehead and a *kadamba* flower at his feet. However, Srikrishna's efforts to kill him continued, and he did succeed finally in sending an emissary who killed him by deceit. Subsequently, he was deified, and the local tradition is that the milk of every cow or buffalo that calves must be offered to him before it is drunk.

There are scores of other gods and goddesses and demons of local origin who are worshipped in the area. Sometimes the distinction between the gods and demons is so slim as to be practically non-existent. Cairns, usually with a piece of iron sticking out of the top, have been erected all over Kumaon. These are intended to ward off ghosts and demons.

The average Kumaoni has little time for daily ritual. Owing to the exigencies of terrain and the general shortage of water, he washes his clothes and has a bath only once a week at the most, or on special *puja* days. However, he is emotionally attached to the *kul devta*, usually the main idol in the village temple, and not one of the major Hindu deities. Golu *devta* has a large following; so have Bholanath, Gangnath, Kalika *devi* and Nanda *devi*. The other gods get attention during their particular `days' or festivals, and during the very special institution of a *jagar*.

The *pahari* belief in the supernatural is the belief of fear that sprites, ghosts and ancestral spirits can affect fate in a malign way. This must be avoided by rites and rituals or prayers which will restore the affected person to health and prosperity. Hence the *jagar* where a *shaman* identifies the spirit or god who has turned his evil eye on the worshipper as a result of which ill health, death or economic misfortune has befallen the family. The *jagars* take place on occasions other than those associated with the festivals of particular deities, and consist of the ceremonial recitation of a long folk poem, detailing the exploits of one particular god or goddess. The recitation can take either a few hours or a few weeks, and is a very specialised ritual as the *jagar* singer is traditionally identified, and each singer restricts himself to only a few themes or stories. Devotees organise *jagars* in thanks-giving (on the birth of a son, for example), or to fulfill a vow or to propitiate a demon who has possessed someone or is deemed to be harassing the family. Incidentally, the harassing demon or deity has to be initially identified by a *dangariya,* an oracle or *shaman*, who is possessed by the deity called up by the *jagariya's* singing and drumming and who henceforth speaks on behalf of the deity. The *dangariyas* are very often women, and he or she is not only the diagnostician but also recommends the treatment — either a *puja* for propitiation, or exorcism in cases where the diagnosis is possession by a ghost. The *jagariya* is never a full-time practitioner as the income from this ritual is spasmodic and unspecified. The job requires years of preparation and there is no system of teaching the profession. Nor is it a hereditary occupation. Any boy who is interested learns by going to as many *jagars* as he can and committing the stories to memory. He also has to learn to play the drum though there is also a traditional drummer or *hurkiya* who can be called upon. Each *jagariya* becomes a specialist and, in general, confines himself to one or two specific deities, whose chants he learns by serving an apprenticeship with a senior *jagariya*. The *shaman*, of course, just has to have a gift. This variety of *Jagar* singing is becoming rather rare these days, and the village people are not very forthcoming in satisfying the idle curiosity of outsiders about these very special rituals.

Of recent years there is a growing tendency to hold elaborate rituals to appease the spirits of ancestors whose last rites have not been properly performed and who, therefore, have brought misfortune upon the family. These rituals can take several days, and in many cases, include animal sacrifice. *Jagar* singing associated with specific festivals (Nanda Ashtami, for instance) is of a different kind and consists of ritual songs sung to the goddess on the day of her festival. These *jagars* last all night, and incidents of possession by other gods take place throughout the ceremony. Bill Aitkin's description of one such *jagar* that he witnessed in Almora has been quoted earlier.

Certain diseases are supposed to be of supernatural origin. Specified practitioners diagnose the illness; others, called *jharnewale*, are supposed to have the power to cause the disease to reverse itself. Strokes, for example, are always treated by *jharnewale*. Men having been identified as having been born *ulta* — breech deliveries — can cure backache. The treatment varies with the disease but it usually consists of the chanting of *mantras*, and then alternately touching the patient and the ground with a feather, thereby grounding the disease.

We have already mentioned that Buddhism was probably dominant in Kumaon in the seventh century. To Shankaracharya is attributed the cleansing of Hinduism and the elimination of Buddhism from these regions. He dispersed the Buddhist monks and nuns, and disbanded the old Baudhmargi priests. Hieun Tsang, the great Buddhist traveller is supposed to have visited Kumaon in 633-643 AD. His mention of Govishan in his writings has been identified as a reference to modern Kashipur.

Muslims in the area are largely confined to the urban areas, and are descendants of those invited into the kingdom by the Chands as *shikaris* to rid the area of dangerous wild beasts, and cooks who would cater to their Muslim and Christian guests. About seven per cent of the Muslims live in the urban centres of Ranikhet, Almora and Nainital. The 0.15 per cent who live in the rural areas are *manihars*, or cultivators. Among the oldest of the Muslim settlers in the area, they also work in horn, and make bangles, these being their traditional occupations. Their customs and habits are indistinguishable from those of their Hindu neighbours.

Christianity came into Kumaon with the British. The earliest Indian Christians were those converted by the London Missionary Society, which came into Kumaon in 1850. It was followed by the American Methodist Episcopal Mission in 1871. Christian communities still exist in pockets near the larger towns in the area. Since there were large contingents of British troops quartered in these hills, especially in Nainital, Ranikhet and Almora, these towns are dotted with very beautiful churches. Nowadays, very few are in use. Unfortunately, the unused churches are gradually falling to pieces, taking with them remnants of beautiful oak pews, lecterns, stained glass windows and old inscriptions which tell us a good deal about the congregations that once thronged these buildings. There were at least seven churches in Ranikhet alone, each catering to a different Christian denomination (Catholic, Church of England, Presbyterian, Wesleyan, Methodist, and so on). Of these only three are still in use. Two have been converted into shawl-weaving centres, and one is devoted to the preparation and the preservation of maps. The others are gently falling apart, and are being taken over by the undergrowth in the oak or *deodar* groves that originally sheltered them.

## Chapter 5

# The Ecology of Kumaon: A Paradise in Peril

The Himalayas are one of the youngest mountain systems in the world and, in fact, younger than many mountain systems even in India. For instance, the Aravalli, Nilgiris and Vindhya ranges in the country are estimated to be 1500 to 2500 million years old whereas the Himalayas are only 40 million years old. Geologists believe that the Himalayas originated in a vast sea basin adjacent to a land mass. There is definite geological evidence that vast stretches of the Himalayas were originally covered, several million years ago, by what was known as the Tethys sea. Even recently, rocks of marine origin of the Cretaceous age (60 to 80 million years ago) have been discovered under the snows of Mount Everest and other great mountains. Rivers deposited vast quantities of sediment into this sea, which started subsiding at the bottom. After perhaps a few million years, the depth of the basin brought it into contact with the hot interior of the earth. This resulted initially in a compaction of the lower layers. The Himalayas emerged from under what was originally the sea mass by a series of 'uplift' phases. These series of geological phenomena ultimately resulted in the sea waters draining away, and the rising mass of sediments rose to form a mountain chain. The different parts of the mountain chain

were thus formed. According to geologists, the Himalayas
are still rising and, therefore, are inherently unstable. In case
the equilibrium of the mountains is disturbed due to any cause,
stresses build up within the apparently solid and strong rocks
until a critical point is reached when the stresses are suddenly
released and displacement of rocks can result. Many
earthquakes are caused in this way in the Himalayan ranges.

Most people think of the Himalayas as ancient and
strong, and in fact as a mighty protector of the country in
the north. In reality, the Himalayan mountains are
geodynamically sensitive, youthful as compared to other
mountain systems of the world, and not particularly strong
in a geological sense. The Himalayas largely consist of weak,
deformed rocks which are severely stressed and easily
susceptible to the onslaught of heavy rains, and the vibrations
and disturbances caused by the movement of heavy traffic
and human interference. The ecological balance of the
Himalayas is very delicate, and any type of developmental
programme has to ensure minimum adverse impact on it.
These mountains therefore deserve great care when
considering excavations, major road-building exercises and
heavy construction. We should also avoid creating further
environmental hazards resulting from the removal of
protective forest and vegetation cover. As we shall see in the
course of our discussion in this and other chapters, the nature
of the Himalayan mountain system has effects on all aspects
of development in the hill areas.

## General Characteristics of Climate in Kumaon

The Himalayas presents a wide variety of atmospheric
conditions, which vary according to the direction of mountain
valleys, alignment of ridges, and relative differences in the
elevation and altitude of the mountain ranges. In fact,
remarkably wide differences are noticed in the Himalayan
region even over short distances. There are broadly two types

of climate in the entire mountainous region. These are designated by climatologists as the *moderate climate zone*, and the *alpine climate zone*. 'Moderate climate' prevails in heights up to 3000 metres. The 'alpine zone' covers areas above 3000 metres where the only inhabited parts are the alpine valleys where large tracts are covered with snow during winters; the alpine hills represent extreme conditions, with a perpetual snow cover. Even in the moderate climate zone, there are variations in the climate depending on whether we are talking of the hills or the valleys. Both pressure and temperature are affected by the altitude, both decreasing as the altitude increases. Rainfall in Kumaon also manifests great variety and is dependent to a large extent on relief features, mainly the nature and alignment of the mountain ranges, and not only on the altitude. To take one example, the average annual rainfall in Ranikhet is less than half that of Nainital though the altitude of the two places does not differ to any great extent. The year is generally divided into three main seasons: the cold season from November to February, the warm/hot season from March to mid-June, and the rainy season from mid-June to October.

## Earthquakes, Erosion and Landslides

The Himalayas have had a few major earthquakes in the last one hundred years, and experts have identified several potential earthquake-prone areas known as 'seismic gaps' where the strain is building up progressively. The Kumaon region itself has had no major earthquake in this century, and the nearest major earthquake in recent years had its epicentre in Agora in Uttarkashi in the Garhwal Himalaya. But the multiplicity of geological faults and the underlying geological instability (referred to by geologists as 'tectonic ferment') in these mountains, hold the ever present threat of danger. In order to reduce the impact of future earthquakes, some experts have suggested the preparation of hazard-zoning maps in which the areas of potential hazard are identified. In addition to potential earthquake-prone areas, Valdiya points out that it is important to identify areas and belts prone to rockfalls, landslides and debris flows on the basis of geological features, rainfall data, past history and current signs of slope instability.[48] This could help in relief and preventive measures to be taken expeditiously at times of crisis, and also to take into account the geological sensitivity of certain areas in the construction of new roads and buildings.

As far as earthquakes are concerned, it is perhaps not possible to do much more about them than to provide relief quickly when they do occur. But as far as landslides are concerned, it is certainly possible to take some preventive action. For instance, every new road or large construction in the hill areas should be examined from the point of view of slope instability and other geological features before going ahead with it. The construction and planning of all buildings must also take into consideration the forces likely to be generated by earthquakes.

While hazard-zone maps may help communities to prepare plans to meet potential earthquakes, the more important daily threat faced in these mountains is that of landslides. Valdiya has pointed out how the geological problems of the unstable mountains have resulted in the gradual but persistent 'uplift' of the terrain, which has significantly quickened the rate of erosion. Precise figures are not given but the present rate of erosion is many times higher than in the immediate geological past, and it is gradually increasing. Such higher erosion has the effect of increasing the instability of the hill slopes.

In addition to this accelerated erosion owing to geological reasons, there is the erosion of top soils because of deforestation and reduction of vegetal cover. The accelerated erosion rate has the consequence of voluminous sediment production, filling valleys and reservoirs. The figures are staggering. In one catchment area alone in these hills, every

The long tailed blue magpie

A cattle-lifting leopard poisoned by the villagers

Musk deer (an endangered species) in Dharamgarh Sanctuary in Almora District

Pink rhododendron which grows between 8000 ft to 10000 ft.

100 square kilometres is reported to produce nearly 23 hectare metres of sediments annually. The sediments take away the top soil rich in nutrients. The process of erosion also weakens the mountains, which become more susceptible to landslides than before. Inadequately planned road construction, haphazard building constructions and continuing deforestation aggravate the threat of landslides. Even during the preceding two years 1998 and 1999, there have been many big landslides in the Kumaon hills. A landslide in Nainital town recently destroyed part of a road on the hillside above the less populated (and undisputedly more beautiful) side of the lake. Another major landslide at night near the border of Pithoragarh district ended in major tragedy, killing more than 200 pilgrims on the route to Kailash Mansarovar. These are warnings and pointers to a grim and dangerous future if timely action is not taken.

It is, in fact, clear to anyone familiar with the Kumaon area that the construction of new buildings does not usually take into consideration environment-related concerns which are genuine and urgent. For instance, under the UP Roadside Land Control Act, any construction within 100 feet of the centre of a PWD road is totally forbidden. Yet one has only to drive a short distance on any of the main roads in Kumaon to see numerous residential buildings and shops very much within this distance from the road, some of them old, but many in the process of coming up without any visible effort on the part of any public authority to stop them. It is difficult to believe that the concerned officials are not aware of these constructions, which are not only illegal but add to the potential instability of the hill slopes. This is truly a man-made and, therefore, avoidable environmental hazard.

There are many such instances of unplanned development which one comes across on a daily basis in the Kumaon hills. Many 'resorts' and residential complexes which are totally unplanned and, in some cases, haphazard are coming up outside the municipalities and cantonment areas. No approval of any authority is required for any construction outside the municipal or cantonment areas, and it is not clear as to what extent considerations of slope stability and related environmental aspects have been taken into account in planning these complexes. The authors are personally aware of one residential development near Ranikhet where regular water supply is not available, i.e. there is no water connection from any rural or other scheme. Many of the houses have been bought by persons from Delhi and elsewhere. Whenever the owners or their guests stay in these houses, which is usually for a week or so during each visit, water for domestic requirements has to be brought in tankers from about twenty kilometres away.

As far as new construction activities are concerned, it does appear necessary to have a 'planning authority' to approve all new constructions in the hill areas so that considerations of slope stability, landslide hazards, water supply, etc. are kept in view. Architects or certified civil engineers familiar with hill construction may be required to certify in the case of each new building that its location, plan and other characteristics satisfy the considerations of slope stability, etc. and that sanitation and water requirements have been taken into account. This may help to restrict haphazard construction activity in the hill areas.

## Water

Water has a crucial role in all domestic, agricultural and industrial activities. The geological instability and ecological sensitivity of the Himalayas as well as the fact of its being the source area of all major rivers of north India gives added significance to the availability and management of its water resources. Prima facie, there ought to be plenty of water in the Himalayan region for irrigation, drinking and other daily requirements. In fact, more than a billion people in four countries — India, Pakistan, Tibet and Bangladesh — depend in one way or another upon water from the Himalayan rivers. But the inhabited Himalayan areas  suffer from a chronic shortage of water, to which theme we will be returning repeatedly in the course of our discussion. Water supply schemes in many villages have become inoperative because of poor maintenance and other factors such as reduced flows in the streams and the springs. A study conducted by Tiwari in the Upper Kosi catchment area, which includes Almora town, showed that only about one-third of the recommended requirement of domestic water supply (120 litres/per person/ per day for urban areas and 90 litres for rural areas) was actually available.[46] The situation is broadly the same throughout the Kumaon hills. Valdiya says: "this 'too little-too much water' syndrome, is characteristic of a desert country."[48] Another writer says that "the perennial problem posed by water in the region lies in this duality — surfeit and scarcity".

The main sources of water supply in the hills are the mountain rivers, which in turn derive their water partly from the melting of snows and glaciers, from the monsoon rains and the hill springs which are analogous to groundwater in the plains. There is an abundance of flow in the Himalayan rivers — which consist of three major river systems, viz. the Brahmaputra, the Ganga and the Indus. It is estimated that these three systems have an average annual flow of 1200 billion cubic metres. For the Kumaon region, the Ganga system is relevant, some of whose major tributaries such as the Kosi and the Ramganga flow through it. The Ganga system alone has an estimated annual flow of 460 billion cubic metres, of which nearly-half can be used for irrigation. This compares very favourably with the irrigation potential of the Brahmaputra basin (a mere 3 per cent) and the Indus basin (about 25 per cent) .

Though some of its major tributaries flow through the Kumaon hills, the main source of the Ganga is the Gangotri glacier in Uttarkashi district in the Garhwal region of the

Himalayas, where it is called the Bhagirathi; the other source
of the Ganga is the Satopanth glacier near Badrinath, where
it is known as the Alaknanda. The two rivers merge at
Devprayag , also in Garhwal, to form the Ganga. It then flows
through Uttar Pradesh, Bihar and West Bengal. During the
course of its 2500 kilometre journey, the Ganga bifurcates
into the Padma (Bangladesh) and the Hooghly in its lower
reaches, flowing into the Bay of Bengal. The Ganga basin
catchment area, which includes its many tributaries, is nearly
11 lakh square kilometres, of which nearly 80 per cent is in
India. The Ganga basin itself covers more than one-fourth
of India.

In Kumaon, the rise in snow-fed rivers occurs from March,
with peak flows in June and July, whereas the rise in rivers
originating below the snow line commences from early July,
peaking in August and September. Generally, all rivers are
in spate during the monsoon season, and 70 per cent of the
total river discharge is noticed in July, August and September.

Because of the nature of the topography and the force
of the water-flow down the hills, the potential of generating
hydroelectric power is considerable in such territory, and the
Kumaon hills are no exception. For the Ganga basin, for
example, a power potential of nearly 11500 MW (at 60 per
cent load factor) was estimated in 1981 though the actual
realization of this potential is still quite small. Of course,
implementation of more hydroelectric power projects could
inevitably bring in its wake various environmental problems.
These potential projects are located both in the Kumaon and
the Garhwal regions. Some of these projects are under
implementation, but the untapped potential is still
considerable.

It must also be mentioned here that the irrigation potential
is largely realizable only in the plains, though additional power
can be utilized anywhere in the grid, including the hill region.
However, it must be mentioned here that the real need of
the people of the hill region is water because the power

requirements of the region are quite small, as industrialization in this area has so far been very limited. From another point of view, however, the new power projects can represent a source of income-generation for the new hill state.

## Springs

Springs and mountain streams are often the only available water source in the hill areas for agriculture, horticulture as well as domestic uses. While precipitation in the form of snow-accumulation on the mountain slopes forms the principal source of water in the higher altitudes, rain water is the main water source in the lower mountain ranges. Rain water adds to the surface flow of the rivers and streams, and also percolates and 'infiltrates' under the ground to emerge as springs. The nature of the soil structure is very important. Infiltration is greatest in the relatively rough, permeable and more gently sloping terrain. Almost all perennial springs and streams are located generally on the 'fault-lines' or 'fracture' of hard impermeable rocks. While there is a vast quantity of water flowing in the Himalayan rivers, most of the water frequently runs down the hills, only to cause floods in the plains. The scarcity of water in the hill region is a real one as there is an enormous difference between water flowing during the dry and the rainy seasons. One expert says that, in streams fed by springs in the lesser Himalayas, the difference may sometimes be more than 30000 times! Even modest estimates put the difference as more than 1000 times in most cases. A spring in the hills is replenished continuously by rainwater seeping through the soil as well as seepage from river water in the surrounding areas. This is known as 'recharge' of the spring water and is somewhat similar to the recharge of the underground water which provides water for tube-wells and pump-sets in the plains. For a spring to have adequate flows of water, the recharge must be adequate and continuous.

Springs where the water is available round the year for
utilization are known as 'perennial springs'. Many springs dry
up during the course of utilization. In fact, more than 85 per
cent of rainwater in most areas flows down the mountain
slopes as surface-runoff, and less than 15 per cent is available
to recharge the Himalayan springs on which large numbers
of hill people depend. Deforestation and poor agricultural
practices have resulted over the years in the reduction of the
water-absorption and retentive capacity of the land. In a field
study of 49 springs done by Tiwari, it was found that 18 had
completely dried up during the last 10-15 years due to these
reasons.[46] Villagers have also reported that the flow in the
remaining springs has reduced considerably during the last
two decades. Greater absorption by the soil will occur if the
vegetation cover increases, i.e. greater afforestation will
reduce the surface run-off and make available more water to
recharge the Himalayan springs.

Augmenting the water flows in the springs by the
development of spring sanctuaries has been suggested by one
expert on the subject. The idea is to enclose the catchment
areas of different springs with appropriate fencing to prevent
access of grazing animals as well as fodder and timber
gatherers. As part of the augmentation plan, trenches and
pits will be made in order to promote infiltration of more rain
water which can recharge the spring water at a greater rate
than before.

## Rainwater Harvesting

'Rainwater harvesting' is a term used to denote the systematic
and regular collection of rainwater basically for domestic use.
In suitable cases, underground reservoirs and dugouts can be
used for storing rainwater. Of course, rainwater harvesting
can be done in the plains areas as well, but it appears to
have greater relevance in the hill areas. Many households
in Kumaon have already started rainwater harvesting from

their roofs and the movement is gathering momentum. Some non-governmental organizations are also engaged in the construction of rainwater storage tanks in the hill areas. Rainwater can be an important source of household water supply for uses other than drinking and cooking. It cannot normally be utilized for drinking purposes as it lacks many essential ingredients necessary to make it suitable for human consumption, but it can be used for bathing, washing, gardening, etc. An ideal way of using rainwater is to gradually utilise it over the dry months from the storage reservoir at a rate that will ensure that the stored water lasts till the inflows in the subsequent rainy season. The collection and storing of the rainwater, if done on a large scale in the hill areas, also means less 'surface runoff' and, consequently, less top-soil erosion.

## Glaciers

Glaciers are formed from the accumulated snow which has survived melting during the summers. When the snowfall during the winter is greater than the quantity of snow that melts during the following summer, a glacier can be formed. One writer on the Himalayas mentions that there is no specific word in Indian languages for 'glacier', though the hill people have local names such as *bamak*, *gal*, etc. A large number of glaciers may be found above the permanent snow line, i.e. 17000 feet above sea level. The formation of a glacier depends on area-specific factors such as the height of ridges, slope-orientation and the quantum of precipitation. For example, on account of differences in the solar radiation, south-facing slopes have usually less ice-cover. Nearly forty years ago, it was estimated that nearly 17 per cent of the Himalayas, i.e. about 33000 square kilometres, were under glacier ice. There are an estimated 15000 or so glaciers in the Himalayas, some of them being 1 to 5 kilometres in length. Some glaciers such as the Siachen, are as long as

72 kilometres, and the Gangotri in Garhwal is 26 kilometres long, but the glaciers in the Kumaon region are smaller. In Kumaon, the Milam glacier is 19 kilometres in length and 3 kilometres in width, and the Pindari glacier is 3.5 kilometres long and 500 metres wide.[20]

As already mentioned, the Himalayan glaciers are also a very significant source of fresh water, a substantial part of which goes into feeding the rivers near their Himalayan sources. An idea of the water potential of a glacier can be had from the fact that Gangotri glacier has an estimated volume of ice which is more than twice the total capacity created by the Bhakra dam. In western Himalayas, of which the Kumaon region is a part, the upper reaches of the major rivers do not get much monsoon precipitation and the glaciers contribute substantially to the river water. The melting of the glaciers contributes more than half of the water flow in many of the Himalayan rivers. But the melt water is often wasted, as least as far as the hill region is concerned, as the melting reaches its peak in the late summer just before the rainy season which follows it very closely. In fact, while glacial melting can supplement a weak monsoon, it can aggravate a flood situation where the monsoon is strong. The melt water, while flowing down the hill slopes, does augment the flow in the Himalayan rivers as well as the springs, but a substantial part of it flows down the slopes as 'surface runoff' and is wasted as far as the hill areas are concerned.

Perhaps because of 'global warming', many glaciers are receding and a vast frozen asset is reducing with each passing year. Observations by some experts support this trend, e.g. the Pindari has shrunk significantly during the last one hundred years while the Milam glacier has 'retreated' by nearly 1.3 kilometres during the same period. On the other hand, some recent studies appear to indicate that some glaciers have begun to increase in size again, which is indeed a hopeful sign.

As the peak period of melting coincides generally with the rainy season, some methods will have to be found to store this melt water by suitable dams at high altitudes, thus enabling the use of this water at the time of need. One expert has suggested glaciological and hydrological investigations for the preparation of suitable water-resource development programmes. It has also been suggested that such dams, as they will be located in very sparsely populated higher Himalayan altitudes, may not cause the environmental problems that similar projects can create in the populated lesser Himalayan areas.

As can be readily imagined, glaciers are a great attraction for those tourists who are interested in trekking in the mountains. They thus form an important part of what is generally called 'adventure tourism'. Specific details of trekking routes and maps are given in Chapter 9.

## Biodiversity

Any discussion of the environment will not be complete without referring to biological diversity, usually termed 'biodiversity', which denotes the multiplicity of life forms which sustain our planet. Biodiversity is the "property of living systems of being distinct, that is, different, unlike." It refers to the variety and variability among living organisms and their surroundings. Three categories of biodiversity, viz. ecosystems, species and genes, are usually distinguished.

Ecosystem biodiversity refers to the variety of habitats in the biosphere; e.g. a landscape which has croplands, grasslands and woodlands has more diversity than another with just fragmented woodlands. Species biodiversity concerns the different species prevalent in a specific geographical area. Genetic diversity concerns the genetic varieties of plants, animals and microorganisms. For example, if an area includes domestic varieties of a crop as well as its wild ancestors, it has more genetic diversity than an environment free of wild ancestors.

Most of the world's biodiversity is found in the tropical zones, and the Himalayas are particularly rich in this respect. Though the mountain range is essentially in the temperate region, the climate ranges from near-tropical to sub-tropical, as well as temperate to the alpine, with the permanent snow-line at high altitudes. This wide climatic variation is substantially responsible for the vast variety of plants, other vegetation, animals and birds in the Himalayan ecosystem. The Himalayas are a rich repository of plant and animal wealth. Western Himalayas (Kumaon and Garhwal) have a cold- and drought-resistant vegetation in many areas, dominated by conifers such as *chir pine*, blue pines, *deodhar*, fir and spruce as well as legumes, grasses and composites. The variety in the altitudes, precipitation, climate and soil types contribute to the biodiversity seen here. The biodiversity is reflected in agriculture, horticulture, forestry and animal husbandry as well as wildlife. The broad-leaved and coniferous forests in the altitudes 300 to 3600 metres are a transition from varieties such as *sal* which dominate the lower altitudes. Western Himalayas have very rich faunal diversity as well. It has been reported that they have over 1400 species of invertebrates and 843 species of vertebrates. The Corbett National Park alone, in the foothills of Kumaon, is reported to have 48 species of raptors such as black-shouldered kite, Egyptian vulture, Eurasian griffon, sparrow hawk, black eagle, etc.; over 500 species of birds, including several migrant varieties, are also reported to be present in the park. In fact, many people are not aware that the Corbett Park, which is usually associated in the public mind with the tiger, is literally a bird-watcher's paradise.

Biodiversity can exist at the level of a population (inter-breeding group of individuals of a species), community (different species in the same habitat) and ecosystems (interacting groups of communities of plants, animals and microorganisms in a climatic zone). If there is no interference from human beings, ecosystems can be self-perpetuating and self-sustaining only with external inputs such as sunlight. Of course, no one can reasonably suggest a total lack of intervention in the ecosystem by the human race. But the interference must be such that both humanity and the ecosystem can survive! This is what is usually called 'ecologically sustainable development'.

Largely, owing to human depredations, some of the species in the Himalayas are facing possible extinction in the near future if remedial and preventive action is not taken. These are known as 'endangered species'. Such species can be in plant life or animal/bird life. The ecological significance of such species is that they are likely to be lost for ever to the world unless deliberate efforts are made to protect them. It is important to protect and preserve endangered species as they are vital for the preservation of biodiversity, which in turn is vital for the integrity and viability of the ecosystem as a whole. Threatened fauna in the western Himalayas include *sambar*, barking deer, *goral,* wild boar, black bear and *kalij* pheasant in the foothills; musk deer, monal and pheasants in temperate areas around an altitude of 2500 metres, and musk deer, snow leopard, snow cock and brown bear in the sub-alpine zone around 3000 metres. Similarly, there are many plant species which are endangered in Kumaon, some of which have high medicinal value. These species are mentioned in Chapter 6.

The need to conserve as wide a genetic base as possible is at the root of the problem of the preservation of biodiversity. The existence of biodiversity in agriculture, for instance, is the basic starting point of all research and development in this sector as well as in the area of drugs and pharmaceuticals. Scientists maintain that it is necessary to guarantee the survival of gene pools existing in the wild species so that constant supply of these genes is available to help insulate agriculture, horticulture, forests, animal husbandry and the pharmaceutical industry from future threats of diseases, pests, etc. Conservation of wild species is therefore an important part of the biodiversity conservation programmes. A large number of plant species have productive potential in the pharmaceutical industry. Many have already been used in drug formulations, and unless this biodiversity is sustained by careful and planned exploitation, posterity may lose part of an invaluable resource.

Apart from innumerable wild edibles (334 varieties in central Himalayas alone are listed by experts) such as roots, tubers, flowers, fruits, seeds, etc., which are nutritionally important, a large number of fodder species exist in the Himalayas. Wood, which is still a major domestic fuel, is dependent on a variety of forest resources which are under threat of reduction owing to several (human) causes. The Himalayan region supports over 80 species in the timber category alone.

Apart from the above, culture collections of a number of Himalayan species of micro-organisms (bacteria, viruses, algae, fungi, etc.) are used in metal and coal mining operations, cleansing oil spills, controlling pests, etc. These are only a few random examples to illustrate the significance of biodiversity.

A good example of a major change in biodiversity in the Himalayas, especially important in Kumaon, is the shift from *banj* (oak) to chir pine forest as the dominant species in many areas. *Banj* has innumerable uses for the hill people. It is a very good charcoal and firewood source, though it is slow-growing. It also provides abundant fodder, being a broad-leaved species. The leaves also generate a thick humus, which is an excellent fertiliser. Its very capability to meet multiple needs has led to its over-extraction for firewood and charcoal, lopping for use as fodder and removal of the humus from the forest. This over-exploitation combined with its slow growth results in poor regeneration and the forest ground being rendered bare. The importance of regeneration of the oak forest is not often realised as the failure of regeneration would not come to notice when the old trees are still there in the forest. It is therefore essential that the programme of dissemination of young oak seedlings is undertaken on a regular basis to ensure continuity of the forest in the long run. In some areas, oak forests are allowed to make way for apple growing and, in many others, to chir pine. The area thus becomes a favourable habitat for chir pine, which grows faster and has some commercial value for the forest department while not being of much use to the local people for fuel, fodder, etc. The shift from *banj* has further consequences for other flora and fauna associated with *banj*, and the whole forest composition changes gradually. Problems of soil erosion, water scarcity and loss of biodiversity invariably result from the loss or reduction of the oak forests.

Biodiversity also faces another threat from the growth of uncontrolled tourism. Many builders are buying land and building tourist complexes which do not often take into account the capacity of the available infrastructure to handle the needs of this extra influx of population. Visiting tourists are known to throw plastic bags and other non-biodegradable material which, in due course, is covered by the autumn leaves. Ultimately, this leads to the plastic material preventing the rainwater from seeping under the soil and augmenting the springs. Plastic accumulation can also prove destructive to the green life on the mountain slopes. The area between 3000 to 5000 metres above sea level, while it covers less than 5 per cent of central Himalayas, is very rich in species biodiversity but tourism and overgrazing have threatened the biodiversity of these meadows. Ajay Rawat has suggested that the extraction of medicinal herbs and plants should be banned in this area.[37]

Biodiversity has a number of values for society, both direct and indirect. The direct values or benefits are obviously related to consumption, but the indirect benefits are more related to existence, keeping the options for posterity, and perhaps even survival of the human race on this planet. The loss of biodiversity is, to some extent, a worldwide phenomenon, but the problem is generally agreed to be most acute in the tropics, especially in the Himalayan region. Biosphere reserves, national parks and wildlife sanctuaries are invaluable in conserving important elements of biodiversity in the Himalayas. The relative importance of the Himalayas is seen by the fact that 6 out of 14 biosphere reserves are in the Himalayan region.

It is essential that the importance of the maintenance of biodiversity in the Himalayas is recognized and accepted as an integral part of development planning. The recent 'biodiversity policy statement' of the Government of India, recognizes this importance.

## Forests and Forestry

Vegetation and forest cover are of vital significance for the economy and ecology of the hills. They absorb water under the land surface, which in turn feeds the groundwater and especially the life-giving springs. They also bind the top-soils through the root systems and stabilize the atmospheric support in regard to moisture and carbon dioxide content, apart from providing energy to productive economic activity, especially agriculture. Forest cover in the hill areas thus performs several vital functions. It protects the slopes not only from soil erosion but also from landslides by binding the soil. It also improves precipitation by controlling the surface flows of water down the hill slopes. This helps to augment water in the springs and the streams.

The mountains and forests have always been intimately associated with one another. While 11.5 per cent of the geographic area of Uttar Pradesh (including the hill districts) is under forest cover, the hill districts alone have 44 per cent of their area under forests, according to official statistics.

Data on 95 out of 98 hill districts in the country shows that 30 districts have more than two-thirds area under forests while the remaining 65 districts have less than two-thirds. All the hill districts in UP fall in the latter category. The figures for Almora, Nainital and Pithoragarh districts of Kumaon, are 47 per cent, 53 per cent, and 39 per cent, respectively (including the newly carved districts of Bageshwar, Udham Singh Nagar and Champawat, which were originally parts of these three districts).[23]

The National Forest Policy, 1988, emphasises the protective function of forests in maintaining ecological balance and environmental stability. It aims to have one-third of the area of the country under forest cover. For the hill areas, a higher figure of two thirds of the area is proposed, mainly "in order to prevent erosion and land degradation and to ensure the stability of the fragile ecosystems" On the basis of this yardstick, the forest cover in the Kumaon hills is quite inadequate. In fact, many observers of the Himalayan scene believe that even the official figures of afforestation cited above are an overstatement of the field realities. An unofficial expert study based on satellite imagery interpretation has estimated that only 28.7 per cent of central Himalayas is afforested and only 4.4 per cent has forests with a crown density of 60 per cent.[40] These are much lower than the official figures.

Forestry practices and policies have been widely criticised for the present unsatisfactory forestry situation in the hill areas. The afforestation and plantation plans have not kept pace with the widespread felling, both by the organised sector for commercial exploitation and by the local peasants for their energy and other needs. It has been pointed out that a tree takes minutes to fell and bring down, but more than fifty year to grow to its full size. S.L. Shah has estimated that, if the present rates of exploitation of the forests continue, natural regeneration will cease by 2031 AD. Similarly, grazing pastures will be exhausted by 2041 AD.[42]

The forestry policies were formulated several decades ago under the assumption of limitless forests meeting the needs of a limited population. This no longer holds good. Now the number of people per hectare of cultivated land in Kumaon, is nearly three times that of the plains of Uttar Pradesh. The population densities (which are much lower for the hills) do not give a clear picture as the cultivated and cultivable land in the hills is a much smaller proportion of the total area as compared to the plains.

The main criticism frequently made of the forestry policies during the period of British rule and later is that they gave priority to commercial considerations over the needs of the local population. The forests were substantially used for timber needs of the industry; *sal*, teak, and *deodhar* were used for railway sleepers, and broad-leaf varieties such as oak (which were useful for local people in various ways, but not so suitable for commercial exploitation) gave way to conifers such as the pine, which were commercially more worthwhile. This emphasis seems to have been continued in the forestry policies in the post-independence period as well. The most striking example of this slant  was the encouragement given to pine forests and the reduced emphasis on broad-leaved varieties such as the oak.

The consequences of rapid deforestation are many. The local populations are facing a firewood crisis, the nutritive top soils are getting depleted, the mountain springs are getting drier and the quickened run-off of the water down the slopes and the mountain rivers leads to floods lower down in the plains. The consequences for agriculture and other sectors have been discussed in an earlier chapter.

## Forest Fires

In recent years, forest fires have caused considerable damage to the eco-system of the hill areas. Forest fires have several adverse consequences. The water springs are not recharged

*Brahma kamal (Saussurea obvallata)* — a high altitude flower which grows only above 13000 ft.

The Nanda-Sunanda procession on the occasion of Nanda ashtami

Girls in traditional Kumaoni dress

The Catholic church in Ranikhet — built in 1899

adequately and they start drying up. Forest growth is retarded, the soil nutrients are adversely affected and erosion is given a further undesirable impetus.

It is not our contention that forest fires were unknown in the past, but there is no doubt that they have increased in recent years both in frequency and intensity. The villagers are usually blamed for most forest fires because they traditionally burn pine needles and pastures after summer to encourage the growth of fresh grass during the rains. This is also done by the villagers to make the grazing safer for the cattle on the slopes by reducing slippery litter. It has been recently reported by many observers of the hill scene that the villagers have developed a hostile relationship with the Forest Department, and do not often cooperate with the officials in controlling forest fires. The hostility arises because the villagers perceive the department as denying them any rights in the forests, which traditionally provided them with fuel and fodder for centuries. While villagers have to be prevented from burning of forests for grass, it is also important to ensure that the 'timber and resin mafia' (to use Ajay Rawat's term) do not set fire to the forests for their advantage and put the blame on the villagers.

## Destruction of the Himalayan Ecosystem

A lot has been written and talked about the gradual destruction of the Himalayan ecosystem and its long-term implications for the country. In the earlier parts of this chapter, we have tried to highlight some of the major ecological factors involved in the process. While we have concentrated on the Kumaon region, most of the problems are common to the entire Himalayan region. We shall now try to summarise these factors and examine briefly what can be done to arrest, and perhaps reverse, some of the adverse trends that have developed over the years.

Both natural and man-made factors have influenced the ecological system of the hills. Natural erosion is a major factor in the Himalayas. The precipitation levels caused by the monsoon (July-September) are without parallel in the world and the effects of heavy rains and water-flows down the mountain slopes of the Himalayas cause considerable natural erosion. The steep terrain, the instability of the young Himalayas and the heavy water run-off down the hills combine to cause tremendous erosion of the slopes. One expert estimates that "if heavy rains double the water-flow, scouring capacity is increased four times, carrying capacity by thirty-two times, and the size of particle carried by sixty-four times".

The natural process is augmented by human interference in the ecosystem. Increased population pressure, excessive exploitation of forest resources, destruction of the mountain ecosystems by terrace cultivation practices, rearing of excessive livestock, certain types of road and building construction, eco-destructive practices of tourists — all of these contribute to this process. The condition and state of the forest cover in the hills have major effects on the capacity of the forest to absorb and retain water, and also on soil quality. A good forest absorbs more water and ensures a lower water-flow down the slopes. When the monsoon is long and intensive, as in the Himalayan region, the condition of the forest assumes major importance. The speed of the water-flows along the slopes also increases when the forest cover is reduced, and this in turn increases the scope for landslides in the hill areas.

## Steps towards a Solution

Hans Christoph Rieger has pointed out specifically in the Himalayan context that "the existence of a problem does not necessarily guarantee the existence of its solution". Many ecologists fear that the impending destruction of the ecosystem of the Himalayas has by now become irreversible. However, we owe it to ourselves and posterity that even at this stage, we make all efforts to arrest it.[20]

In reaching towards a solution of the Himalayan ecological problems, we must recognise the policy limitations clearly. We have to identify those variables that can be influenced by the government's policy measures and decide on suitable policies to influence them in the right direction. For instance, while we cannot affect the monsoon in any way, we can mitigate to some extent the intensity of the water run-off by structures such as check dams, river bank consolidation, etc. Similarly, population control measures may slow down future population pressures in the hill areas and elsewhere. Human behaviour in the areas of forestry, construction, irrigation, cultivation and terracing practices can be suitably influenced by various policy measures in order to mitigate adverse environmental effects. Alternative fuel for domestic uses could reduce human incursions on the forest for firewood. More rapid afforestation is another long-term measure that is definitely a feasible policy approach to counteract the deforestation that has gone on for the last several decades.

Listing out some of the possible policy approaches, as we have done, brings out clearly the monumental nature of the problem. The problem is also substantially social, as evidenced by the behaviour of the hill population in all environment-related matters. An economist would say that this is a typical example of the difference between the individual and social points of view. From an individual's point of view, the felling of a single tree does no great harm but benefits him and his family immensely in the short run. But if each of a thousand individuals cuts a tree, it results in the destruction of a forest. What can be called *future-ignoring behaviour* manifests itself in the cutting or lopping of trees in the public domain. The requirements of the next generation appear very remote to the current generation which is overwhelmed by the problems of day-to-day living.

A similar case of ignoring social costs is seen in the decimation of public-owned forests. After all, if A does not fell (illegally, of course) a particular common-owned tree, perhaps B or C will do it. So it is privately rational for the first man (A) to cut and utilise the tree himself even though it imposes costs on society as a whole. The persistence of indiscriminate grazing in a publicly owned forest which needs a regeneration period is another such instance. If A does not graze his cattle, B or C would be likely to do so before he does so. It therefore makes (private) sense for A to grab the grazing opportunity before the others do so. But it is undesirable socially.

Therefore, what is required to resolve 'this dilemma of collective action' is either mutual agreement or coercion, or a little of both. This dilemma is best explained by the concept of the 'isolation paradox' first popularised in economic analysis by Amartya Sen long ago in one of his early books. This visualizes a situation where A may agree to a certain common policy restriction or measure *provided* B, C and all the others agree to it, but A individually will not agree to follow it himself. In the forest case, this would mean that A will agree not to cut trees in the common forest provided he is reasonably sure that B, C, etc. can be prevented by law or common agreement from doing so. This obviously would provide adequate justification for community action and active intervention by the government in conserving the forest wealth.

The role of public policy and effective intervention by the state and the central governments are therefore evidently crucial in the task of arresting the degeneration of the Himalayan ecosystem. The task is both figuratively and literally Himalayan in its dimension and scope. There is need for public awareness of the extent to which human interference has affected the Himalayan environment, and how this will affect not only the hill areas but the entire country for generations to come. We must take action before it is too late. As one writer on the Himalayas has observed graphically — "there is only one Himalaya to lose".

*Chapter 6*

# The Kumaon: Flora and Fauna

The Himalayan range extends over an area of 500,400 square kilometres of which the Kumaon region accounts for only about 25000 square kilometres. Yet it is difficult, if not impossible, to give a comprehensive or complete account of the flora and fauna of even this limited area. In addition to topography, climate and altitude, which are primary factors in deciding these matters, natural factors such as soil erosion, landslides, floods, avalanches and forest fires bring about major changes in vegetation and, consequently, in animal, bird, insect and reptile life.

Expanding population, defence perceptions after the Chinese war of 1962 and developmental activities have led to extensive road building and construction activity in the entire Kumaon region. Bill Aitken says in his book *Mountain Delight*:

Jim Corbett repeats on every page how well-wooded the slopes of Kumaon were and how dangerous it was to pass along the thickly wooded ridges when the light began to dim. Now almost all the main ridges have motor roads, silent after the sole daily bus has passed along. There is no sound of the wind in the trees for the trees are mere

90

poles. The leaves have been hacked for feeding buffaloes, the branches chopped for fuel.

He adds ruefully:

All I know is that Kumaon was a green and pleasant land twenty years ago and today it is a blasted heath ruined by well-intentioned planners in the name of hill development.[2]

In addition, new varieties of crops and plants have been introduced to satisfy the needs and desires of a new generation of people. Trees like the willow and the eucalyptus, and fruit-bearing plants like the apple, peach, cherry, pear and other temperate varieties have been planted. The interior of the region has been opened up to commercial plantations.

These factors have had a negative effect on the natural flora and fauna of the area. The need to open up more areas for cultivation has led to the firing of undergrowth and the felling of old forests. The slow-growing oak has been extensively cut down for fuel. Each oak forest destroyed takes with it a large number of varieties of ferns and orchids, and the rich, damp soil that supported it becomes arid and dry. The quick growing pine replaces it. The pine is majestic in its own way, but pine forests are prone to forest fires and not as effective as oak as binders of the soil and conservers of moisture.

Commercial and sociological factors are now becoming increasingly important as factors that govern plant life in the region. But natural factors like the direction of the hill slope, the amount of protection afforded from the cold north winds, the amount of sun they get and the level of precipitation can change the nature of the plants and shrubs that grow in a particular area. For instance, in the authors' north-facing garden in Ranikhet, exposed as it is to the icy winter winds sweeping down from Trishul and Nanda Devi ranges, the infant citrus plants are frozen to death every year. A friend across the way, whose garden is on the southern slope of the hill, grows lemons and sweet lime by the basketfuls. And he is only two hundred yards away.

Broadly speaking, plant life in Kumaon follows certain patterns, largely governed by the altitude. The Tarai and Bhabar forests of the foothills still support exuberant monsoon forest growths of *sal, sain, haldu, dhanri, khair (acacia catechu* which yields *katha) amaltas (cassia fistula)* and *semal (bombax malabaricum), tun* and b*auhinia variegata.*

These deciduous forests of the foothills are a rich mosaic of colour, especially in spring and early summer, when the red silk cotton or semal, the *dhak (erithina)*, the dark orange 'flame of the forest' *(butea frondosa)*, the golden *cassia* and the *kadam* dot the variegated greens of the area. *Sal* dominates these forests, for it is vigorous and hardy, and sometimes attains a height of 30 or 50 metres. *Sal* is the most important tree in the Himalayan foothills as it is used for railway sleepers. Beyond the *sal* forests, the undergrowth thins out and only the *screw pine* exists to remind us of the tropical nature of these forests. In addition, a tree fern of the variety known as *hemistelia*, which looks like a palm, and another genuine palm called the *fish tail* or *sago palm* are to be found here.

Between 1,000 and 2000 metres above sea-level, there is a preponderance of the *chir pine*. This is what we largely find in places like Almora, Ranikhet, Binsar, and so on. Above this height, there is a fair growth of *banj oak, rhododendron* and *deodar* in addition to the pine. The *banj oak* is the most valuable variety of tree to be found in this area, but where a forest like this lies near human habitation, it is usually heavily degraded because of extensive lopping for firewood and fodder. The best *banj oak* forests are developed in moist-shady depressions in sheltered areas. There is also some *silver fir*, and *karshu (quercus seme carpifolia)* to be found here.

*Pine* is omnipresent in these forests, and is of many varieties. Chir pine, for instance, is found in the lower altitudes often inter-mixed with *sal*. In the higher reaches it occurs along with red *rhododendron* and *banj oak*. Even higher, at heights of 2000 to 3500 metres, *chir pine* gives way to *blue pine* (*pinus wallachia*) which is the variety that coexists with *deodar* and *fir*. A third species of pine, *chilgoza pine* (*pinus gerardiana*), is found in the dry inner ranges along with *juniper* and *deodar*. A characteristic of a pine forest is that the number of pine needles falling on the forest floor prevent extensive undergrowth.

At altitudes of between 2500 and 3500 metres, *moru oak* (*quercus floribunda*) which flourishes at about 2400 to 2800 metres gives way to the high altitude *karshu oak* (*quercus semecarpifolia*). *Moru oak* grows alongside red *tree rhodendron* (*rhododendron arboreum*) and requires cooler conditions than *banj oak* and grows best in areas which have heavy snowfall in winter, while *karshu* grows at a higher altitude and is associated with *blue pine* and *yew*. The leafy canopy in a forest of *karshu oak* is usually very heavy, and often individual trees attain a height of 20 metres or more. At the upper limit of this zone, the high level fir also makes an appearance.

These mixed forests of oak and conifer support a particularly thick undergrowth. This encourages the retention of moisture during the rainy season, and so we have a large number of *mosses*, *lichens* and *ferns* as well as flowering plants and orchids.

*Rhododendron* of different varieties also adorn the snows of winter above 3000 metres, though these do not attain the growth of the varieties at lower reaches, as those at higher altitudes are mainly shrub varieties. The bright red *rhododendron* which adds to the glorious views of winter, especially after a snow fall, gives way at higher altitudes to pink and white bush varieties. Birch (*bhoj*) is found at a height of 4000 to 4500 metres, and its bark provides the *bhoj patra*, which served as paper in mythological times. Juniper grows extensively here, but above this height the main and, in fact, the only vegetation to be found is green *algae*.

The higher reaches of the mountains are also home to the flora of temperate Europe. *Edelweiss, gentians, anemones, potentillas and primula* abound. The famous blue poppy, considered by many to be the most beautiful flower in the Himalayas, grows at a height of 3500 metres. The remarkable fact about efflorescence at the higher reaches is that these flowers have to perform, within the space of six weeks, the entire cycle of growth, flowering and seeding, while at heights below 3000 metres, they can spend three or more months to go through the same process.

Plant and flower life in the Himalayas varies according to altitude, the depth of ground water (if any), the amount of rain they receive and the direction they face. A grassy flower-clad valley can yield, within the space of a few kilometres, to a rocky and barren hilltop. A few hundred yards in another direction can lead to a hillside or pasture land, covered with an entirely different species of flora.

Each season has its own flowers, and though efflorescence is heaviest in the early spring (March-April), and the monsoon (July–August), even winter has its blooms.

It is thought that the western Himalayas have upward of 7,500 species of seed plants and are among the richest areas of floral and faunal diversity in the world. One reason for this rich variety is that the Himalayan range is probably the youngest in the world, and though it had its beginnings under the ocean, it has never again been subjected to submersion or extensive continental glaciation, unlike other mountain ranges. As a result, not only have many older species survived but newer varieties have also evolved.

In recent years, the G.B Pant Institute of Himalayan Environment (at Katarmal in Almora district) has done extensive work cataloguing the medicinal plants used locally in Kumaon. The exhaustive list details not only the botanical and local names of the plants but also the area in which they are largely found, and tells us the ailment for which local people use the plants. It reads like a homeopathic pharmacopoea. For example:

*Aconitum balfourii stapf (ranunculaceae)* L. *meetha bish.*

A rare herb, it grows on shady moist slopes of alpine pastures between 3500-5000 metres.

Uses: Root paste is used in sepsis, boils; roots are eaten by human beings to develop body resistance.

*Osimum sanctum (tulsi)* is infusion of leaves used in malarial fevers.

Many species, like *rauwolfia serpentina* and *taxus wallichiana* which are extensively used in allopathic medicine (and in fact have revolutionized medical treatment), are Himalayan in origin. Other important medicinal plants are *dioscorea deltoidea, atropa accuminata, podophyllum hexandrum, nardostachys grandiflora. Digitalis spp. ioscorea*, found at an altitude of 900 to 3300 metres practically all over the Himalayas, is used to manufacture steriods; *atropine* is used to dilate the pupil of the eye and comes from *atropa. Podophyllum*, or the Himalayan *mayapple*, is a high-altitude plant at 2500 to 4500 metres and is used in remedies for skin cancer. Similarly, *digitalis*, or *foxglove* is a major component in medicines for cardiac complaints, and *rauwolfia serpentina* is used in cases of chronic hypertension.

## Wildlife in Kumaon

There is an extensive variety of wildlife in the region, though poaching and the shrinking of natural habitat and tree cover threaten many species with extinction.

The Corbett National Park in the foothills of Kumaon, though plagued by poachers, still manages to provide a very good cross-section of the animals that earlier roamed

unhindered all over the Tarai region. Many varieties of deer
roam freely in the sanctuary — *sambar*, spotted deer, hog
deer and *kakar* or barking deer made so famous by Jim
Corbett in his stories. Made fearless because of the protection
afforded to them, many of them come up to the car and stare
unafraid through the windows.

Large herds of wild elephants are easily visible in Corbett
Park, especially in spring and summer. Carnivores such as
tigers and panthers are still to be spotted, but not too easily.
Either their numbers are diminishing in spite of Project Tiger
or they have become more wary. Panthers are plentiful, but
as they are very nervous of encroaching on tiger preserve,
they are confined to the upper reaches of the park (above
1,000 metres) where tigers are not found. Wild boars roam
in herds as do jackals. Pine martens and foxes abound as do
many varieties of monkeys and wildcat species, including
interesting varieties like the leopard cat. The rivers swarm
with alligators, *gharials* and otters as well as many varieties
of fish. Bird life in the park, as everywhere else in the
Kumaon, is plentiful. In fact, the park is an orthinologists'
paradise, some of the exotic species to be found there being
the bird of paradise and the hornbill.

Jim Corbett, who lived in the Kumaon, has recorded for
us, very vividly, not only his adventures while pursuing man-
eating tigers but also the life of the people and the animals
of the area. In *Jungle Lore*, writing of his boyhood in
Kaladhungi in the Tarai, he describes his wanderings in the
jungle, and he says:

> The jungles on both sides of the stream were teeming
> with game in the way of red jungle fowl, pea fowl, deer
> and pig that crossed the game track on their way to or
> from the fields.[13]

These same jungles were the haunt of tigers, panthers and
pythons. Unfortunately this situation no longer exists, and
we have to hope that the reserve named after this great

*shikari* and naturalist will be able to help restore to the region some of its earlier plenitude.

Most of these animals, except for the tiger, are found higher up in the mountains too. The species of panther most readily spotted in areas above 1,000 metres is locally called *kukkur bagh*. Slightly smaller than the panther species found in the plains, it likes to eat dogs. At the same time, it is strong enough to kill and carry away domestic cattle when it is unable to find its natural prey. Reduction of forest cover has caused it to increase its depredations in the villages and, as a result, this beautiful animal, once so plentiful that the Forest Department had classified it as 'vermin', is now rarely seen. Harassed villagers tend to eliminate it by poisoning the kill with pesticide. The panther dies when it returns to its kill, but it takes a long time to do so, and it dies in agony.

The valuable musk deer found between 2,000 and 3,000 metres is very much at the mercy of poachers because the Japanese value its musk pods for their (unproven) aphrodisiac appeal, and the French want musk as a base for their perfumes. The price of the musk pod is higher than that of gold. Though only the male musk deer is in demand, poachers trying to trap it also indiscriminately wipe out the females and the young ones

The Himalayan black bear, also found at this altitude, is infinitely more dangerous than any of the big cats. In fact, Jim Corbett's stories have some interesting descriptions of fights between bears and tigers, always started by a bear poaching a tiger's kill and, when challenged by the rightful owner, attacking the tiger, quite unafraid. There is a belief among the local villagers that, if you meet a bear, you must run downhill, because the bear finds it easier to run uphill than down.

The brown bear is the largest carnivore in the Himalayas and is well provided with fat for its winter hibernation periods. It eats pretty nearly everything, from rodents to domestic sheep and goats and carrion. It is devoted to its young which are born during its periods of hibernation, and devotes considerable time to the upbringing of its offspring. M.K. Ranjitsinghji describes how he once watched a mother bear trying to rest in the afternoon, while its cub ventured out on forays against its mother's wishes:

> Five times she had to bestir herself and bring back the errant cub. Calls and even cuffing was of no avail. Ultimately she half lay upon the cub, one huge arm pinning it to the ground, while it howled in protest. After a while she let it go, whereupon, thoroughly subdued, it curled up beside its mother and went to sleep.

If they could desist from attacking domestic cattle, bears would be safe from hunters, as bear meat and skins have no market value.

Above the snow line dwells the rarely seen snow leopard, and the varieties of the sheep and goat families that are its natural prey — *thar, ghoral* and *bharal*. The shaggy *thar* clings to the safer habitat of cliffs and rocky surfaces, but the *bharal* prefers open ground unless disturbed, when it leaps for the shelter of the crags. Both varieties of mountain goat, however, are extremely curious — a quality that has helped to decimate their numbers, as they easily fall prey to unscrupulous *shikaris*.

The snow leopard is elusive and rarely seen, not only because of its protective colouring but because it dwells in such inaccessible areas that the eager viewer is too exhausted to notice it by the time he reaches its domain. Only people who have taken up residence in the inhospitable terrain that it inhabits have managed sightings (the Bedi brothers who have a film on the snow leopard stayed in the region for several months). The snow leopard is not white but varies from cream to grey, with flashes of rosettes. It is only about three feet long, but gives the impression of greater length because of its bushy tail, which it can use as a wrap-around blanket. Its habitat ranges from 4000 metres to 6000 metres and *bharal*, which is its chief prey, is usually to be found up to an altitude of 5,000 metres. The danger to the snow leopard comes not only from poachers in search of its pelt so highly prized in the world of fashion, but also from the problems that threaten its food — wild goats, *thar*, *bharal* and *ghoral*. These have been reduced in numbers through being hunted for the cooking pot and also because domestic sheep and goats have been introduced into their exclusive habitat by an exploding population of sheep herders looking for fresh pastures. The *bhotia* sheep dog follows these domestic animals and disturbs the *bharal* ewes, sometimes harrying them till they miscarry. Military air manoeuvres on the Himalayan border can cause the wild goats to stampede to their deaths. Deprived of its natural food, the snow leopard (which has been sighted in and around the Nanda Devi sanctuary) faces extinction, a fate that the Snow Leopard Trust, along with the Indian Government, is trying to find ways and means of preventing.

These forests are overflowing with monkeys, the largest and commonest variety being the *rhesus macuaque*, which prefers to live around human settlements. The other variety found here is the common *langur* or *Hanuman monkey*. Both varieties of primates inflict considerable damage on fruit and crops, and the villagers keep their large *bhotia* dogs to protect their crops from these pests. Religious sentiment protects monkeys from traps and guns.

Since the forests of Kumaon are tropical forests, reptiles abound — monitor lizards, pythons and many other varieties of snakes of which the *krait*, the *cobra* and the *Russels viper* are the poisonous species. Of these, the most impressive (and dangerous) is the king cobra or *hamadryad*, another species mentioned often by Jim Corbett. There are also several varieties of harmless tree and grass snakes, sighted quite frequently in the monsoons..

.An unusual snake is the Himalayan *pit viper*. Since it is bright green on top, it looks very much like the grass snakes, but it is classified among the poisonous varieties. The Indian rock python is found mainly in the foothills, where it lives in caves, clefts in rocks, and abandoned burrows. It lives on warm-blooded animals, and is even capable of swallowing large animals like deer, jackal and wild boar. It feeds only once every few days, and invariably becomes very sluggish after a meal. As it has beautiful markings, it was widely hunted for its skin, which was used to make shoes and handbags, but trade in snake skin has now been banned.

Of the 287 species of bird life of the Indian hills described by Salim Ali, 230 species are to be found in the western Himalayas. Like the flora, bird life varies with altitude and season. Perhaps the commonest of the birds, and the most beloved because of its cheerful, early morning song is the dark blue Himalayan whistling thrush. Jim Corbett has this to say about this songster:

> The privilege of catching the early worm is claimed by the Himalayan whistling thrush, better known as the whistling school boy. While walking through the Kumaon jungles in the half light between day and night, or night and day, a bird will flit by on silent wings pouring out a stream of golden song which once heard will never be forgotten.... Morning and evening he pours out his song while in flight, and during the day he sits for hours in a leafy tree whistling in a soft sweet minor key a song that has no beginning and no end.[13]

One of the most spectacular (and probably the most destructive) of birds is the red billed blue magpie, which vies with the monkeys in making depredations on the fruit trees.

Partridge, wildfowl and *chukor* scramble up and down the hillside, conservation laws having made them relatively safe from the cooking pot. Sunbirds and flycatchers are as colourful as the flowers they frequent, and flights of parakeets wheeling in formation at sunset are a marvellous sight. Raptors glide above the valleys and forests, occasionally

Baijnath temple in Katyur valley which houses what many consider to be the most beautiful Parvati image in the country

The Jageshwar temples. One of the twelve Jyotirlingas in India is located here

The Dhwaj temple in Dwarahat — probably damaged in an earthquake

Kumaoni woman at work

coming out of a stately glide to swoop with swift ferocity on their unwary prey.

The two most fascinating birds of the Himalayas are both raptors or birds of prey — the *golden eagle* and the *lammergeier*. Yet another large Himalayan raptor is the bearded vulture, which is found between 1200–4000 metres and is sometimes seen sailing majestically even above 7000 metres. These birds are not only magnificent specimens but are very rare. Little is known about their status and ecology because they live at great heights — above 2000 metres — and in frequently desolate country. The lammergeier is, however, known to carry up huge bones — the femur of an ox, for instance — which it then drops on to rocks from a great height, splinters it and then feeds on the marrow and bone fragments.

However, according to Salim Ali, the phasianidae-pheasants, jungle fowl, partridges and quail, collectively known as 'game birds', may be regarded as the most distinctive bird family of the Himalayas. Some of these are among the most fascinating and gorgeously plumaged birds in the world, and have therefore been victims of poaching and smuggling, which have seriously reduced their numbers. However, they breed freely in captivity, and so there is a hope that captive bred birds can be reintroduced into the wild. The best known Himalayan pheasants are the blood pheasant, the tragopan or horned pheasant, the monal or impeyan pheasant, the khaleej pheasant, the koklas and the chir pheasant. The mountain quail, a smallish bird, slightly larger than the grey quail, is an elusive and little-known member of the quail family. The last known sighting of this rare species was in 1876, and there are only ten specimens available in museums in the UK and America. All of these were collected in areas around Mussoorie in Garhwal, and *Sher-ka-danda* peak near Nainital. The species is so rare that there is a feeling that it has already become extinct.

An interesting facet of bird life in the Himalayas is that many species come in from across the mighty mountain chain to escape the rigours of the central Asian plateau. Some of these, like the ducks and cranes, follow the river valleys and come down into the Indian subcontinent.

Many mountaineers have claimed to have seen birds flying straight across the high Himalayas, even at 8000 metres or more. But these statements are hard to accept, though the first Indian expedition to Mount Everest found three dead steppe eagles at a height of 7900 metres, and Tenzing, one of the conquerors of Everest, found a dead eagle on the South Col in 1952. However, sophisticated modern tracking devices and radar have now conclusively proved that this type of migration does definitely take place.

A number of bird species breed in the higher Himalayas and move down in winter or even fly away to the Vindhyas and the Sahyadris to winter there. The water bodies in the lower Himalayas attract many species of migratory birds from Siberia and the central Asian deserts, at about this same period.

The forest policy of the government has naturally had some impact on the flora and fauna of the area. Little is known about the forest policy prevalent before British occupation except that a custom existed of planting *deodar* trees near temples — Jageshwar is a good example of this. The forests were then extensive and rich and considered inexhaustible. The economy of the hill people depended entirely on the forests for fuel, animal fodder, medicinal herbs, leaf litter for manure, etc. and the abuse of forest reserves was considerable because they were considered inexhaustible.

By 1824–25, these depredations were extensive enough for Bishop Heber to write:

Great devastations are generally made in these woods, partly by the increase in population, building and architecture, partly by the wasteful habits of travellers who cut down multitudes of young trees to make temporary huts and for fuel, while the cattle and goats which browse on the mountains prevent a great number of seedlings from rising. Unless some precautions are taken, the inhabited part of Kumaun will soon be wretchedly bare of wood, and the country already too arid will not only lose its beauty, but its small space of fertility.[5]

The formation of the 'Kham', the extension of railways and the consequent depletion of *sal* forests (*sal* wood is largely used for making railway sleepers) and the resettlement of refugees have destroyed the rich life of the tropical Tarai forest. Commissioner Traill attempted to reverse this process by his forest settlement of 1823. There was great public agitation against this reservation of forests, and subsequent legislation modified his settlement policy considerably. Finally, three main classes of forests have evolved in the Kumaon region — reserved forests, civil forests (protected forests under the administrative control of the Collector) and panchayat forests.

Of recent years, we find that Bishop Heber's predictions have come true to a large extent. Huge landslips, especially in Nainital (where uninhibited and unrestricted construction work has weakened the mountain side) are attributed to careless human activity. However, restrictions on quarrying and tree-felling have helped in the regeneration of forests. New forest projects and schemes now try to enlist the co-operation of the villagers in order not only to protect the existing forests but also to educate them in the fact that this resource which provides them with cattle fodder, fuel and fertiliser is not inexhaustible. Interestingly enough, villagers are no longer resentful of forest officials who patrol the area and control lopping. Their ire is directed at big contractors who fell trees for commercial purposes.

New forest projects which involve the cooperation of NGOs are attempting not only to save the existing forests from further depletion but also to bring more hill areas under forest cover. At the same time, the various animal sanctuaries which have been established not only protect special species but also provide a safe haven for other birds and animals, and with their strict rules, help to educate tourists in the importance of protecting the animals which live in the area. The Corbett National Park near Ramnagar is the best known of these reserves, and is associated with Project Tiger, which has received considerable hype. This park has been described in some detail in Chapter 9 of this book. Apart from Corbett National Park, there are a few other smaller wildlife reserves in Kumaon. The Ascot Musk Deer Wildlife Sanctuary, located in the higher regions of Pithoragarh district, is meant to conserve the musk deer and its habitat. This rare species of deer is at risk because of the musk pod that the male of the species carries, and which is valued as an aphrodisiac and as a base for perfumes. It is not really necessary to kill the deer to extract the musk pod, but poachers are not interested in the preservation of the species, and also kill the females and the fawns in their senseless orgy of slaughter. This sanctuary covers an area of 284 sq. km. The principal forest types found here consist of several varieties of *oak — banj, moru karshu, deodar, fir* and *spruce, blue pine* and, since it covers the higher altitudes, it is also home to *birch* and *fir, rhododendron*, both tree and bush varieties, and *alpine scrub*. Apart from musk deer, this sanctuary houses leopard, jungle cat, civet cat, barking deer, serow, ghoral and brown bear. The Binsar wildlife sanctuary is near Almora, and encompasses an area of about 50 sq. km. This reserve too houses a similar variety of high altitude species, including the musk deer and the khalij pheasant.

Wildlife preservation, as of now, is trying to achieve its aims by persuasion in the hope that the *shikaris'* desire to nab a trophy with a gun may give place to a more innocuous satisfaction in capturing it with a camera, but in this, as in everything else, it is not the lone (though no doubt anti-social) hunter wanting some wild meat who is causing the damage. It is invariably big business that is doing the damage — the sellers of the musk pods, or the dealers in tiger bones and tiger and bear fat, who have no interest in trying to preserve a species. It is, therefore, not education or persuasion that will stop them. It is only heavy punishment. Till fairly recently, the man found with musk pods in his possession was not punished. He was punished only if caught in the act of poaching, and occasions when people were caught in the act were few and far between. Possession of banned articles must now become a serious offence.

Similarly, there are animals that are disappearing because their habitat is disappearing. The snow leopard, for instance, is being eliminated because its natural prey, the *tahr* and the *ghoral,* are being decimated by the sheep dogs that follow local shepherds into their habitat. It is essential that alien species are not introduced into national parks so that the balance of species is not upset.

Many varieties of plants are also becoming extinct because of careless plucking and, more particularly, because of goats which graze indiscriminately and poison the area around with their saliva. Some of these are of medicinal value, plants like *aconitum heterophullum* (*atees*), *rheum emodi* (*dolu*) *dioscorea deltoides* (*kin, gun, shingri mingri*). Some of these fast-disappearing plants are flowering plants of rare varieties — *podophyllum hexandrum, lilium wallichianum, gentiana kurooa.*The damage that this careless destruction can do to our world is incalculable and very difficult for the lay mind to comprehend. The only way to preserve our natural heritage seems to be to cordon off specific areas where the endangered animals and plants are to be found, to enforce strictly the laws against grazing and poaching in these areas, and to punish encroachers and law breakers in the strictest way. The enforcers of the law, forest wardens, rangers, have to be motivated to do their duty, either through indoctrination or through fear of punishment.

Making the public 'aware' of the fragile state of our ecology is just not enough. We have all heard about the fashionable wildlife lover who comes to a fund-raising for the protection of the snow leopard in a *shatoosh* shawl and snake skin shoes, or the macho young man who goes straight out and kills a couple of peacocks to serve to his best friend as a suitable dinner.

*Chapter 7*

# The Kumaon Regiment

Ranikhet, the most beautiful hill station in the Kumaon area, is home to one of the most illustrious regiments in the Indian Army, the Kumaon Regiment. The Army plays a very large part in the economic and social life of this region, and Army service is a major source of income for the Kumaon families. Yet, strangely enough, this famous regiment which gave the Indian Army three of its Chiefs of Staff, and its first Param Vir Chakra, was not even born here. Some of its battalions were raised in Hyderabad, Deccan, as long ago as the closing years of the eighteenth century. The Hyderabad contingent assisted the British East India Company in its battle against Tipu Sultan of Mysore.

Henry Ramsay, who was British Resident in Hyderabad in 1811, started the reorganization of the troops using as a nucleus, two regular battalions of the army of Muhammad Salabat Khan, Subedar of Berar. These battalions have now descended to us as the fourth and fifth battalions of the Kumaon Regiment. Soon after, the first and second battalions were raised, and were originally called the Russel Brigade. This new army of Deccan was first used against the *Pindaris*, bandits and freebooters, who terrorised Central India from 1812 to 1818. In 1853, the Nizam's contingent became part of East India Company's forces. The Hyderabad Contingent was involved in the suppression of the revolt of 1857, and some units also took part in the third Anglo-Burmese War in1885. After 1857, the governance of India was taken over by the British Government from the East India Company, and the Army was further reorganized. None of the units of the present Kumaon Regiment were involved in World War I except to provide replacements for heavily injured British Army battalions.

The process of Indianization of the Army started after the First World War at the instance of the Indian National Congress. After 1919, a small group of young Indians, selected to make sure the background was suitable, was sent to the Military College at Sandhurst. The Fourth Kumaon was one of the battalions selected for Indianization, and two of the Chiefs of the Indian Army belonged to it — Gen. S.M Srinagesh and Gen. KS. Thimayya. World War II started in September 1939. The Indian Army was sent into action as soon as war clouds gathered over Europe. The segment of the Kumaon Regiment, called 4/19 Hyderabad, moved into Malaya soon after the Japanese entered the war. At the fall of Singapore, most of them were taken into captivity. Other battalions were involved in fighting the Japanese on India's eastern frontier and in Burma.

On 27 October, 1945 after World War II had ended, the name of the regiment was changed from the Hyderabad Regiment to the Kumaon Regiment and 27 October has after that been celebrated as Kumaon Day. In 1946, Colonel S.M. Srinagesh became the first Indian officer to command the Kumaon Regimental Centre. Partition and independence brought with them their share of troubles in the shape of communal riots, which involved the Kumaonis in internal security duties. By the time order was restored in 1947, the Kumaon Regiment went into action in Kashmir. In October 1947, an irregular *lashkar* consisting of 5,000 tribesmen marched into Kashmir. Maharaja Hari Singh at once signed the instrument of accession with India, and the Indian Army was rushed in to save the state. The Battle of Badgam, one of the most decisive battles of the action which saved Srinagar, was fought two miles away from the airfield. A heavily outnumbered company of the fourth Kumaon regiment led by Major Som Nath Sharma held off the enemy until reinforcements arrived, and the airport was saved. Independent India's highest decoration for gallantry, the Param Vir Chakra, was awarded posthumously to Major Som Nath Sharma. The subsequent battle of Shalateng ensured that the irregular tribesmen were defeated and pushed out of the territory. Military activity in Kashmir continued till 1948, and the Kumaon Regiment, notably the Fourth Kumaon, was the one largely involved. Enemy activity in the Jammu area continued for a long time afterwards. The ceasefire between India and Pakistan came a minute before midnight on 1 January, 1949.

In May 1948, the Kumaon Regimental Centre moved from Agra to Ranikhet — a very practical move as it brought the Centre into the heart of the recruiting ground. Major General Thimayya was appointed the Colonel of the regiment at this time.

Two new battalions, Fourth Gwalior Infantry and the Indore Infantry, were also merged with the Kumaon Regiment. General Srinagesh of the Kumaon Regiment became Chief of Army Staff in 1955. He was followed by General Thimayya in 1957. Hostility between India and China was sparked off by the Chinese occupation of Tibet in 1959, though much provocation had been caused earlier by China's construction of the Sinkiang-Tibet road through Aksai-Chin. This action meant that the Chinese laid claim to 12,000 square miles of Indian territory — barren, waterless, uninhabited territory, but Indian territory nonetheless.

The war with China in the autumn of 1962 saw the Kumaon Regiment involved in the hostilities on the eastern frontier as well as in Ladhakh. In fact, Major Shaitan Singh of Thirteenth Kumaon bathalion received his Param Vir

Chakra posthumously after the battle of Rezang La in which C Company was wiped out. Brigadier T.N. Raina, also of the Kumaon Regiment (later to be General Raina, and Chief of the Army Staff) received the Mahavir Chakra for his defence of Chusul. The unilateral withdrawal of the Chinese army was as inexplicable as the initial attack. After this war, it was realised that treaties are no substitute for defence preparedness. The strength of the army was doubled, and it was given more and newer arms and ammunition.

In 1965, Pakistan, encouraged by the way the Indian Army had crumpled against the Chinese, attacked once more in Jammu and Kashmir. Initially, they sent in irregular troops, *razakars* and militants, intending to follow this up with regular army troops. Five battalions of the Kumaon regiment were immediately rushed into action in Kashmir. Of these, the Eighth and Fourth were to move to Belgaum from their positions in Kashmir, but heavy shelling began when they were having farewell dinner and they rushed into action instead. The war then reached the Punjab front, and more Kumaoni battalions moved in. The fighting in this sector was particularly heavy as the Pakistanis were fighting to save Lahore. A few battalions concentrated on guarding our border with China.

A ceasefire was effected in six weeks time, and the Tashkent agreement forced the two countries to revert to the positions occupied by them before the hostilities began — to India's great disadvantage.

In 1971, a Naga Regiment was raised in Ranikhet, consisting of both Nagas and Kumaonis. Though they were affiliated to the Kumaon Regimental Centre, the Nagas retained their traditional weapons and customs. The war for the liberation of Bangladesh in 1971 saw several Kumaoni battalions heavily involved in the area as well as in Jammu and Kashmir, Punjab and Rajasthan but, with the ceasefire on 17 December of the same year, this war also came to an honourable end.

The Indian Peace Keeping Force in Sri Lanka in 1987-1991 saw the Kumaonis occupied in that country. Subsequently, the regiment was occupied with fighting militancy in Jammu and Kashmir and in the north-east, a task that still is a major part of its duties. This involvement exploded into full-scale war-like activity in the summer of 1999 in the region of Kargil.

The Kumaon Regiment is the pride of the area. Practically every family there has some male member(s) working in the army. Most of the elderly villagers have done their stint and retired, and recount with pride how they were on duty in Army House or the President's House, and went by 'holicupter' to Assam or Arunachal Pradesh. Simple villagers sitting in the sun on a cold winter's day can tell you more about trekking in high altitudes, and the necessity of acclimatization and how to deal with high altitude pneumonia than highly educated sophisticates who talk about the pleasures of trekking in the Himalayas. This knowledge, experience and a substantial part of their income derive from their involvement with the Indian Army.

*Chapter 8*

# The People of Kumaon: Their Life Style

## The Sociological Structure

The structure of sociological relationships is important in determining the underlying motivations, incentives and disincentives of any society, and we shall, therefore, devote some attention to it here. The caste structure in Kumaon, in fact in all of Uttaranchal, is fairly straightforward. Also, it is not as rigid as the system is in the plains. There are four main caste divisions. The `Bith' or upper castes consist of the Brahmins, Thakurs or Kshatriyas and Khasis. The Doms are the lowest caste. The superior castes consist of Brahmin and Kshatriya immigrants from Maharashtra, Rajasthan and the plains of Uttaranchal who were allotted land by virtue of the services they performed for their rulers, but who showed their enhanced status by not working it themselves. The Khasis came into the region before the high caste immigrants and always remained tillers of the soil. The Doms were probably the original inhabitants of the area, and traditionally performed the more menial tasks. This last category incorporated about thirty sub-castes in all and were the artisans or *shilpkars* — the blacksmith, the carpenter, the shoemaker, the weaver, the tailor, the basketmaker, and so on. Strangely enough, the drummer and the musician who performed into this category, perhaps because they had to touch leather. The *shaman*, however, is not caste-bound.

There were various sub-castes even among the 'Bith' or upper castes, these categories deriving mainly from their occupation. For instance, the highest sub-caste of the immigrant Brahmin was the *Chauthani*, who derived his status and prestige from the fact that he did not perform routine priestly duties but was given an administrative position. The *purohit,* however, was looked down upon because he had knowledge only of matters pertaining to religious ritual. A Khasi who assisted a Brahmin in the performance of his priestly duties could, if he had acquired sufficient knowledge of the required rituals, become a *Khasi Baman*. However, migration from one caste to another was perfectly possible till the beginnings of British rule, when the economic changes initiated by the new rulers hardened the caste system.

The Thakurs or Kshettris were immigrant Kshatriyas who were allotted their castes on the basis of their occupation. The administrative posts being the monopoly of the Brahmins, only a few Thakurs managed to enter their ranks, but here again a certain amount of upward movement was originally permitted. The founder of the Taragi clan was a *sudra*, but was allotted the Kshettri caste because he wielded political power. The majority of the present day Kshettris, however, are the descendents of Kumaoni royal houses. The Khasi-Jimdar was the lowest Bith class because he was an agriculturist and worked with his hands.

During the reign of the Chand Rajas, Doms were not allowed to own land. The upper castes were allotted land, but it was considered undignified for them to cultivate it, so it was given to Khasis to cultivate for them. Before 1947, an agriculturist of the upper castes could extend his holdings by cultivating land hitherto unworked. The caste system changed significantly during the British rule not because the British interfered directly with it but as a result of their other developmental activities. The Doms were now allowed to own land. Metalled roads opened up the interior. Slavery and the selling of human dependents was abolished. British administrators, army officers, missionaries and planters ate beef, eggs and mushrooms. As a result, only Doms would work for them, and thus they came in contact with a culture that made them dissatisfied with their traditional social status. Education and administrative positions now became open to all. The stranglehold of caste, at least officially, began to dissipate.

However, social movements emanating from the plains move slowly up the hills. Brahmin and Thakur villages are still separate. The Doms have a distinct *mohalla* of their own as well as separate water sources. In the village where the authors live a Brahmin family has been allotted a separate plot of land by the village elders, three kilometres away from the main village. A Kshatriya of the village married a Dom girl, and was allotted yet another plot which, however, reverted to the village when the couple decided to wend their separate ways. No Brahmins live inside the village, and when religious rituals have to be performed, the priest comes from another village 15 kilometres away. Since the *pahari* is not given to conspicuous consumption, the distinction between rich and poor is not very apparent. The upper castes do not work with their hands, but hire labour to do manual work. The primary economic activity in the village is agriculture. Then comes animal husbandry. Oxen are maintained in order to pull the plough, and the owner makes money hiring it out in the ploughing season. Cows and buffaloes provide the milk and manure. Buffaloes are more valuable as they yield more milk and it is of better quality, but few people keep them as they are harder to care for because they are heavy and awkward and cannot be sent out to pasture. We were told the story of how an ambitious milkman in our village bought a buffalo from a neighbouring village, and tried to bring it home. It came up to the bottom of the hill, and then got stuck. It stayed there for three days and nights until the other villagers took pity on its hapless owner who had spent 8,000 rupees, and came to his rescue. Four men pulled, three pushed, and three hours later, the buffalo reached the top of the hill, which was only about 500 feet higher. Though buffalo milk is acknowledged to be more nutritious, it is considered that it dulls the brain — 'If you drink too much buffalo milk you will get buffalo wisdom.'

Goats and sheep are also kept, primarily for sale in the market as well as for the manure they produce. Goats are also sacrificed in the temples on special occasions. Illegal economic activities assist some villagers to fill their pockets — distilling illicit liquor is one such activity. So is the growing and selling of marijuana and the felling of trees.

Hill women are probably the hardest worked anywhere in the world. "Our lives are nothing but work," a young girl told us recently, when we congratulated her on her engagement. "Now I work in my parents' house. After my marriage I will work for my in-laws. If I am lucky they will feed me well". Her fiancee worked in Delhi, but had no intention of taking her with him. In fact, he agreed to get married only because his sisters had got married and left the house, and his mother needed help.

The 'money order economy' ensures that most of the men work elsewhere, either in the army or in government service or as domestic servants in the plains. The main burden of tending the fields and livestock falls upon the women. Men do the ploughing of the fields, but sowing, broadcasting of fertilizer, hoeing and weeding is done by women. So is reaping, winnowing, threshing and stacking and preserving of the stalk for later use as cattle fodder.

Of course, the women cook and care for the children, cut grass in the monsoon and stack it to be used as cattle fodder in the winter, and collect firewood. They also collect

pine needles to be spread as winter bedding for their cattle
(it makes excellent manure later), take care of the manure,
dry it and store it. They help in clearing the land, and in
building and repairing the houses. The girl children help in
all this, and one or two of them are usually involved in
pasturing the village cattle by taking them into the forest to
graze. In spite of screeds written by activists on the subject,
their seems to be no possibility that this life style will change
in the near future or that the village women will have an easier
life to look forward to.

This, however, is not to say that the *pahari* woman is
weak, servile or miserable. Most of them are proud,
independent and aggressive. In spite of malnutrition and
overwork, the average *pahari* woman can work every day
in the fields, deliver a baby there and bring it home in the
evening, or tackle a bear with her sickle if needed. A divorcee
can be married again with little fanfare or ceremony,
especially if she is a good worker. Polygamy is also fairly
common, especially if the man has plenty of land and
livestock, or if there are no children by the first marriage. It
is also quite common for these households to be fairly
harmonious. Widow remarriage is encouraged and though
*paharis* are critcized for permitting this by plainsmen, whose
customs about widow and divorcee remarriage they are now
trying to copy, the *pahari* is quite unrepentent about this.
Also *pahari* women of all castes enjoy a degree of freedom
unknown anywhere in the plains. They go wherever they
please, alone if need be, and  are confident and free of
speech. In fact, a heart-warming early morning  sight is to
see groups of cheerful, chattering village women armed with
sickles and ropes, climbing up the forested hillside to collect
grass, leaves or wood, or to find them returning in the early
afternoon, heavily laden, but as cheerful as ever. When one
of them was asked, "What are you going to do now?", she
laughed and said: "Work. Cook, clean, milk the cow. What
else do we ever do?"

Girls selling Kaphal (a wild fruit)

Somnath Parade ground — named after Major Somnath Sharma (Kumaon Regiment) the first Param Vir Chakra in the Indian army

Anashakti ashram — Mahatma Gandhi wrote "Anashakti Yoga", a commentary on the Gita, during his stay here

Nainital Lake

## The Bhotiyas

The hill tribes who live in the high Himalayas, on the border with Tibet, are collectively known as the Bhotiyas. There are different sub-groups of Bhotiyas and, though they all share a semi-nomadic culture and provide a buffer between Indian and Tibetan culture, the tribes are quite distinct culturally depending on whether they live in Kumaon or Garhwal, and how they have developed economically.

The Bhotiyas are very obviously of Tibetan origin. Their facial features as well as their language bear strong witness to this fact, but Bhotiya tradition maintains that they are of Rajput origin; that initially they lived south of the great snowy range; at some period they moved across the mountains and into Tibet, but after several generations, they came back and re-established themselves in the higher reaches of Kumaon-Garhwal.

The main concentration of Bhotiyas is in the Mana and Niti valleys of Chamoli in Garhwal. These are called Marchas. Those who live in Uttarkashi are called Jadhs, and the Bhotiyas of Pithoragarh are Shaukas, Darmas and Byans. All Bhotiyas, in general, live in villages which lie at a height of 3,500 metres and, as these heights are not conducive to agriculture, they have evolved a semi nomadic lifestyle where they move to villages lower down the mountains in winter.

The Bhotiyas of Pithoragarh, like those in other parts of Uttarakhand, were non-agriculturalist, and the areas in which they lived were always deficient in foodgrains. Before the war with China in1962, their most important occupation was trade with Tibet. They imported salt, borax and wool from Tibet in exchange for foodgrains, cloth, sugar and miscellaneous household articles. This trade occupied them during the four summer months, and then, in winter, they travelled down to the north Indian markets to sell their Tibetan acquisitions and buy goods for further trading. Local (*pahari*) gossip has it that the Bhotiyas traded Indian salt for Tibetan gold-dust — a kilogram of salt given for a kilogram of gold-dust received — but this perhaps is one of those pleasant myths, more wish fulfilment than fact. Initially, the Bhotiyas owned the land in the villages to which they migrated in winter though they did' not cultivate it personally. Their tenants — Brahmins, Kshatriyas and Harijans — cultivated it for them and were paid wages for their labour.

After trade with Tibet was stopped in 1962, the Bhotiyas attempted to shift to agricultural pursuits, but unfortunately for them, tenancy legislation deprived them of the land they owned in the lower regions which was now given to their erstwhile tenants. They retained the lands in the upper mountains, but this was insufficient to provide them with a living. Many Bhotiyas were reduced to penury, and have taken to trades like carpet weaving  in order to make both ends meet. The educated among them have joined the services. These changes in their economic condition are bound to affect their culture also.

## Kumaoni Art

Kumaon has distinctive art forms of its own. Early examples of rock painting abound in the area. A recent find is that of the rock paintings in Barechhina, a short distance from Almora, on the Pithoragarh road. Most of these paintings consist of stylized geometrical motifs or human  and animal figures, painted in black, different shades of red and white.

A traditional form of painting that persists is *aipana*, done mainly by housewives. These are designs or motifs painted on walls, door sills, floors, etc. for decorative purposes, especially on festive occasions. These designs have no ritual significance, but another category of *aipana* designs are reserved exclusively for religious occasions and are painted on the *chowkis* or ritual seats. When these are meant for human beings — a bridegroom, a youth undergoing a thread ceremony, etc. — an elaborate pot and foliage motif is used, but when they are meant as seats for idols, *tantrik* diagrams are used, such as the *mandala*, the *swastika,* and so on.

A third variety of *aipana* painting consists of *pattas* or strips depicting elaborate patterns and mythological scenes. These are usually painted on walls, but sometimes paper and wooden sheets are also used.

*Aipana* painting is an art, the intricacies of which are passed down from mother to daughter. Many of the designs, especially those relating to rituals, are not displayed to outsiders at all. Like all traditional arts, it is a dying one, but fortunately some societies and groups have now been formed with the intention of reviving it.

The base on which the Kumaoni *aipana* is made is a bright red ochre colour on which the design is painted with white rice paste, the artist using her fingers to do it.

*Ramgvali* painting, on the other hand, is done on muslin cloth which is first dyed a bright yellow. The pigments used are various shades of red.

Another traditional form of painting is *kunaula* which is a long scroll containing a horoscope and religious texts, all of which are ornamented with elaborate motifs.

Sculpture in metal as well as stone, some of it dating back to the third and fourth century AD and found all over the region, is displayed in the G.B. Pant Museum in Almora. There are some terra-cotta exhibits also.

Passing through Kumaoni villages, you can still see doors, door frames and wooden pillars of *likhai* work — delicate wood carving. This art too has been swamped by cement, mortar and brick, but attempts are being made to revive this ancient craft.

## Dance and Music

*Pahari* living is hard. The terrain, though beautiful, is inhospitable and takes a heavy toll of those who try to wrest a living from it. The average Kumaoni has come to terms with this existence, and has his/her own way of enjoying himself/herself within the precincts of the village. Kumaoni folk dances and music have a distinct character and lilt, and are very much a part of the Kumaoni's daily life.

The dances can be either religious or recreational. Those of a religious character are centred around the worship of the Pandavas, Narasimha, Nirankara or Ghantakaran, and the most popular of these are *Jhora*, *Chanchari*, *Chapeli* and *Devtali*. *Jhora* is a festive dance in which both men and women participate. It is held to honour a god or goddess, the most popular of the deities being Shiva, Durga, Nanda or Kali. The participants hold each others arms and bend forwards slowly, while moving in a circle. *Chanchari*, which is danced at fairs, has small groups of dancers forming semicircles in tune to the music, and is slower than *Jhora*. These two dances are variants of the basic ring or circle dance of the Himalayas. The number of participants can swell to a hundred, if required.

While *Chapeli* is a lover's dance of swift movements, accompanied by songs relating to love, romance and adventure, *Devtali* presupposes that the gods themselves are participating in the dance. *Dhol* is danced in the temples, and has no accompanying music. As the name suggests, it is danced to the beat of the drum.

Of the dances performed for recreation, the most popular are *Bhado*, *Cholia*, *Kyunki*, *Jhumaila* and *Chaunfula*. *Bhado* celebrates the deeds of local heroes and kings. *Cholia* and Kyunki are swift stepping dances reserved for marriages and *melas*, the former danced by men and the latter by women. The end of the harsh winter and the coming of spring is celebrated with the group dances, *Jhumaila* and *Chaunfula*.

The music of the region too is suited to the occasion. Marriages call forth *Shakunkar* and *Mangal* songs though we find that, with the spread of cinema culture, film music vies with these lovely old tunes these days. *Neoli* tunes are supposed to be duets between lovers, one on a hill top and one in the valley below. The beautiful plaintive notes float down the hill sides, quite often when the women of the village climb up to cut grass and while away the hours with music. *Chaitis* are meant to be sung in the month of Chait (April-May) at a particular festival when gifts are given to married sisters. *Bhagnolas* are romantic songs, the lines of which are first sung by the lead singer and then repeated by a chorus. *Bairas* are frequently extempore, in the shape of dialogues, sung by two groups or singers. The *hurkiya bol* is a song sung by the village drummer or *hurkiya*, to the beat of his drum, with which he lightens the labours of his fellow villagers while they are sowing the seed or harvesting the crop.

The old customs are fast dying out, especially in the villages near the motor road but, thankfully, the Kumaoni tradition of singing and dancing on religious and festive occasions, and at fairs and *melas,* still persists. Songs sacred to particular deities are part of the specialised knowledge of *jagar* singers, who are still called upon to perform when a household is plagued with bad luck or ill health, and suspects it is because of the malign influence of a god or goddess. These songs are passed on to any young man who desires to take on the profession, but each *jagariya* specialises in only one deity. And often, even now, the plaintive notes of a flute float down the hillsides, probably played by some village youngster who has taken the sheep or cattle of the village to graze and is beguiling his loneliness.

### Folk Art

The folk art of Kumaon, like that of the rest of India, takes its themes and motivation from religion. *Aipana* — floor decoration, *bar-boond* — wall patterns, and *jyonti* and *patta* figure drawings are arts that are primarily household ones. The skills are passed on from mother to daughter, and the materials — rice ground with water, wheat flour, dry earth colours and some vegetable dyes — administered using the tips of the fingers, the fist or the palm, are absolutely domestic in origin. The *aipana* is applied on the courtyard, on the steps leading to the main door, on the threshold, the floor or seat of the *puja*. The floor is first smeared with red paste, and then the *aipana* designs are traced on it with white rice paste. *Bar boond* means dots and dashes. The traditional designs consist of a particular number of dots (24, 29, and so on are auspicious numbers) joined together with dashes, and the resultant patterns are filled in with different colours, the main ones used being red, vermilion, green, yellow and violet. A *patta* is a two-dimensional image of a particular deity, drawn on the wall or on a sheet of paper for a festival or a ceremonial occasion.

*Dikaras* are clay images of particular deities made of a mixture of clay and cotton. They are then coloured white with rice flour mixed with water and then painted with earth colours. These are the figures that are made for Harela, for instance.

### Festivals and Fairs

When we talk of festivals and fairs, we concentrate only on those celebrated by the Hindus because the other communities are in such a small minority that their celebrations have no public impact. In general, all the Hindu festivals are celebrated in the Kumaon, but there are a number which are very special to the area. One of the chief Nature festivals celebrated in Kumaon is *Basant Panchami,* which marks the coming of spring. Winter is long and hard in the region, and it is quite natural to look forward to the end of the season, with its frosts and sleet and bone chilling cold. As soon as the buds swell on the trees, and the first green tendrils begin to break, Basant Panchami is celebrated with great enthusiasm. The young girls of the household crown their elders with tender shoots of barley, and everyone wears yellow clothes and dyes all the cloth in the house yellow — bedsheets and handkerchiefs particularly. By the second week of March, the peach and the rhododendron are in full bloom, and the birds are chirping merrily. *Phooldeyi*, or 'the flowers on the threshold' is celebrated at this time. The day before Ram Navami, for instance, is called *Chaitranavratra*, and is held sacred to the Devi. Similarly, Vikhauti in mid-April is the season for fairs of great importance held in Dwarahat, Sealdeh, and Lohaghat. In fact, the months of March-April are enjoyable months for the villagers as festivals and fairs follow hard upon each other, and there is much merrymaking. Harela, or 'the festival of the rains', the most popular festival in this area, comes soon after the rains start and is dedicated to Gauri, Siva, Ganesha, Kartikeya and innumerable village godlings, including Golu Devta. About ten days before the actual festival, five kinds of grain — usually barley, wheat, mustard, gehot and maize — are mixed and sown in small baskets containing earth. These are watered everyday till they sprout. On the day before the festival, they are weeded with a mock hoe, and as many kinds of fruit as possible are heaped up along with the young shoots. Clay images of Siva and Parvati are placed in the baskets exquisitely fashioned and colourfully painted. The mistress of the house then worships them, reciting a Sanskrit *mantra*, requesting the gods to remain forever in the midst of the family's fields and take away the sufferings of their devotees. On the next day, the master of the house cuts down the green stems, which are then worn by young and old alike. The girls of the house then anoint the men with the red *tika* and rice, and the rest of the day is spent in merrymaking. *Wallgiya* or *Ghi Sankranti* is observed on the first day of Bhado when the fields and the cattle are flourishing. The villagers give curds and vegetables to all their elders and to people who have some sort of authority over them — tenants to their landlords, artisans and craftsmen to those who may be potential buyers, wealthy men of the village and those in authority over them. They are given gifts in cash or kind. *Rakshabandhan* is the occasion to ratify the ties of brotherhood, but is also celebrated with a fair in Devidhura in honour of Varahi Devi. *Krishna Jayanti* and *Ganesh Chaturti* are followed by *Naga Panchami*, which is as important here as it is in Maharashtra, though in more northerly areas of the plains this festival is not really known. After this comes Nanda *Ashtami*, the most important festival in Almora and in parts of Garhwal. The Nanda Devi pilgrimage, which has been described elsewhere, starts on this day, which marks the end of the Devi's annual visit to her *mait*, and the start of her journey back to the harsh land which is her *sasural*. *Khatharuwa* marks the arrival of winter. Huge quantities of hay are heaped up all over the village, particularly at heights. Immediately after sunset the bonfire is lighted, and children and boys armed with cucumbers and flowers arrive on the scene. They throw bits of cucumber and flowers into the fire and jump across it. A story in Kumaon says that the festival began when a Kumaoni king ordered fires to be lighted on every hilltop, to convey to Almora the news that he had defeated the king of Garhwal in a battle. Interestingly enough, the story that prevails in Garhwal is exactly the opposite — the king of Garhwal had fires lighted to signal his victory over the Kumaonis. In any case, the festival definitely marks the beginning of winter. Quilts and blankets are taken out and sunned, and invariably come into use the very next day. *NavRatri*, *Durga Puja* and *Vijaya Dashmi* are marked by extensive celebrations, the Kumaoni *Rama Lila* being celebrated with great enthusiasm not only in Kumaon but by all *paharis* exiled in the harsh plains. Since this is essentially an army dominated area, *Dasehra* is marked with the ceremonial sacrifice of goats. *Kojagar*, a minor

Diwali, comes several days before the real Diwali, and the gambling with which the favour of the goddess Lakshmi is sought begins on this day. The day after Diwali is *Govardhan Puja*, when the cows, which are so important to the villagers, are bedecked and worshipped. *Yamaduitiya*, or *bhai dwij*, is the day after Goverdhan Puja. *Makar Sankranti*, 14 January, is followed the next day by a festival for children, when they are garlanded with edible toys made of flour and sugar. The festival is also called *Uttarayani*, and is marked by bathing fairs, the most important being the one in Bageshwar. Since Shiva 'belongs' to this area, *Shiv Ratri* is very important, and has most of the local people observing fast in honour of their mountain deity. In addition, of course, there are the regular festivals of the Hindu calendar, all events which encourage the abbreviation of the arduous village chores, and find scores of women walking off to the nearest town to participate in the small *melas*, and worship in the temple. Apart from these, there are *jatras* or mass pilgrimages to Dunagiri near Dwarahat in April, and to Jageshwar in the monsoons.

## Marketing Fairs and *Melas*

The hill areas have developed their own marketing methods, keeping in view their problems of terrain, transport and climate conditions, as well as the human population over a vast and sometimes inhospitable territory. While fairs, especially cattle fairs, are not unknown in the plains, hill fairs have a flavour and importance that are uniquely their own. Most of the fairs are annual events, and generally coincide with some religious festival or season. Many of them are held in the valley areas where there is usually adequate space for the vendors to spread their wares, and the buyers from far and near to gather in some comfort. With the increasing road transport network and owing to many other reasons, many fairs are slowly losing their importance but many are held regularly in their appointed places every year. We have tried to give a brief account of some of the more important and colourful fairs in the Kumaon.

Bageshwar, till recently part of Almora district, and now the headquarters of a new district, is a town at an altitude of 100 metres above sea-level. *Bageshwar Mela* is one of the important annual fairs which commences one day before *Makar Sankranthi* day in mid-January and lasts five days. This fair has been held for as long as local people remember, perhaps for one hundred years or more, and is by far the biggest fair in the Kumaon. It is estimated that around 20,000 people from many surrounding and some far-off areas assemble here on these days. Some of them — the intending buyers — stay for a day, and many of them for more than two days. Of course, the vendors arrive a day or two before the fair commences, and most of them leave on the last day. A wide variety of articles of daily use are sold in the fair, but domestic animals, implements and clothing have traditionally dominated the transactions. The Bhotiyas, who have always been nomadic tradesmen, usually bring blankets, shawls and carpets as also Bhotiya ponies, goats and sheep. Many of them also sell wooden bowls, medicinal herbs and leather or skin bags. Traditionally, *ringal* mats and baskets have been brought by Danpur traders, who also sell iron and copper vessels. The traders from Almora, which is the nearest reasonably large town, have dealt in cotton goods, umbrellas, utensils of various kinds, grain, oil, salt, sugar, soaps, toy watches, belts, torches, imitation jewellery, etc. Neighbouring villages bring milk, curd, fruits, walnuts, etc. As in many such fairs, religious tradition plays a role, and many of the visitors take a bath before the fair at the confluence of the Saryu and Gomti rivers.

The Bageshwar fair is not all trade and business. The lighter side is provided by the camp fires, singing, dancing and gossiping that goes on all night for some of the visitors.

Over the years, the fair has lost some of its popularity because of the increasing road network, which progressively reduces the importance of such events. However, it appears that the fair will continue to take place regularly, though the scale and variety of the trade transactions may well decline in the coming years. Who knows — it may well become an attraction for tourists in the future!

The *Jouljibe* fair is held at the confluence of the two rivers, the Kali and the Gori. This is much nearer the Nepal border, and hence has its own special characteristics, such as the dominance of cross-border trade. Jouljibi is at the junction of four important routes — Nepal, Askot, Johar and Darma. The Bhotiya and Nepalese traders traditionally came from the border with ponies from Tibet. Woollen goods, including Chinese rugs, used to be major items of trade in the past and are slowly losing their relative importance over the years. The Nepalese have usually traded in ghee, grain and fruits.

Some 15000 people from many parts of the hill areas assemble in this fair, which has always been held in mid-November since 1914. The Jouljibi fair has no religious significance, but the merrymaking has been reported to be more varied than the Bageshwar fair, with Nepalese and Bhotiya dances being a major feature in the past.

S.D. Pant, writing in 1935, mentions other fairs such as *Devidhura, Vykiasen, Sialde* and *Somnath* in which the emphasis was more on merrymaking than on business. One of the major games that were played was that of sham warfare by hurling of stones at a predetermined target by the competing teams.[31]

As mentioned earlier, the fairs have been losing some of their commercial importance over the years mainly because the increasing number of roads in the hill areas has reduced the need for such itinerant trade and shopping. It would indeed be a loss if the rich and attractive traditions of these fairs is totally replaced by less attractive modern variants in crowded towns.

*Chapter 9*

# Tourist Attractions of the Kumaon

In 1832, Thomas Skinner wrote of the Himalaya:

> ... we entered an enchanted garden, where the produce
> of Europe and Asia — indeed every quarter of the world
> was blended together. Apples, pears, pomegrenates,
> figs and mulberry trees .... I have beheld all the
> celebrated scenery of Europe which poets and painters
> have immortalized. I have seen it surpassed in these
> ... unknown regions of the Himalayas.[17]

Writing on a trip to the Kumaon and other areas in the
Himalayas, undertaken in 1914, C.F. Meade wrote:

> ... in travelling out to the Alps from England there is a
> certain amount of disappointment, for at no particular
> moment can the mountains be said to begin; one reaches
> them by imperceptible degrees. In the Central Himalaya,
> on the other hand, the foothills rise from the plains with
> a suddenness that takes one's breath away.[21]

The Himalayan mountains have always evoked such awe
and admiration from travellers and visitors all over the world.
These hills have always been a great attraction for tourists

**128**

of various types both from inside the country and abroad. From ancient times the Himalayas have been the haven for saints and savants to an extent that they are popularly known as *deo bhoomi* (holy land). But it was only during British times that the hills became a tourist attraction in the real sense. The British developed many hill stations as summer resorts, and some of them, like Simla in Himachal Pradesh and Nainital in the Kumaon region, became summer capitals for the bureaucracy to operate in a more salubrious climate in the long hot summers. Gradually, as communications improved and transport facilities developed, the hills became good places to visit even during other parts of the year for different categories of tourists. In this chapter, we have tried to describe briefly the different tourist attractions of Kumaon. For the trekking enthusiasts, we have given details of the various trekking routes with suitable maps. Of course, some of the temples described in the chapter are tourist spots in their own right, and well worth visiting for their architecture as well as their religious significance.

## The Towns

Kumaon is notable in the Himalayan region for the number and beauty of its lakes. Of these, the best known is Nainital, the town which is named after the lake and which is also the best known of the hill stations in this area. Its main attraction is the lake around which, on the surrounding hills, lies the township. The lake was discovered' only in 1841 by P Barron, who made an extended trip into the hills of Garhwal and Kumaon at this time, and who was astonished to find that a place like this with:

> ... abundance of wood, of the finest water, of level ground, and other requisites for building to any extent; capabilities for miles of beautiful roads for riding and

driving, ... with a magnificent sheet of water both for
ornament and for use, where the manly exercise of
rowing and sailing might have been indulged in ....
was so totally unknown to other Europeans.

He says that the natives showed great reluctance to guide
him to it, pretending that they did not know anything about
it, which he felt was palpably false, as "on the level ground
a fair was held every year, and evidently one of great
resort".[32] He thought it was probably because Nainital was
a lake of such sanctity that the local people did not want
it polluted by the presence of strangers. He was also told
by European officials in the area that the natives had been
encouraged to keep the lake a secret by Traill, the late
Commissioner of Garhwal who, "it is well known, possessed
the most extraordinary influence among the natives of the
hills, and entertained peculiarly illiberal ideas regarding the
influx of European visitors into the Province". Though
Barron attributes this feeling to Traill's jealousy, the fact
of the matter is that Traill was an administrator with an
acute sensitivity to the people amongst whom he worked
and he probably realised that giving publicity to the
existence of this beautiful lake would result in its being
snatched away from the people of the area, which is what
has really happened. Traill was probably the first European
to come to the lake, but the 'discovery' by Barron led to
its development.

Initially, this lake was surrounded by pristine forest,
which, after its 'discovery', gave place to extensive
construction. Many of the old British buildings still exist
and are well maintained — Government House, Ramsay
Hospital, the Nainital Club, the Boat House Club, and so
on. Above Bara Bazar lies the Church of St. John of the
wilderness, one of the earliest buildings in Nainital, and
the finest church in any hill station in India. It was named
by the Bishop of Calcutta in 1844. Though it has been

neglected, and the metal plaques and memorials it contained have been stolen, there is still some impressive stained glass which is worth seeing. The Methodist Church and the Church of St. Francis on the Mall are in a much better state of preservation. Gurney House, which belonged to Jim Corbett, still exists, though it has changed hands several times since then. Some of his trophies are still kept there.

The ancient temple of Naina Devi stands on the flats at the edge of the lake. The old legend says that when Siva and his consort were insulted when they went to the sacrifice held by the latter's father, Daksha Prajapati, Parvati immolated herself. Enraged by grief, Siva picked up her body and danced a wild dance all over the world. Her eyes fell out at the edge of Nainital lake and the temple was built to commemorate the spot.

The town of Nainital was a more beautiful place till deforestation and excessive construction destroyed its *deodar* and pine forests. Fortunately, a court order has banned further construction, and it is to be hoped that this has been done in time to save the town from further devastating landslides.

Nainital is surrounded by seven hills — Ayarpatta, Deopatta, Handi-Bandi, Cheena Peak, Alma, Lariakanta and Sher-ka-danda. Cheena Peak makes a popular day trip. A view of the Himalayan peaks is only available from the hill tops of Cheena, Deopatta and Snow View, but Kilbury, Dorothy's seat and Land's End are popular picnic spots. There are also several walks, especially those on the side opposite the crowded Mall up to Government House and the well-known schools, Sherwood College, St. Josephs, All Saints, St. Mary's, along Sleepy Hollow and the University, and beyond the Nainital Club.

Other resorts near Nainital are Mukteshwar (2286 metres), Ramgarh (1789 metres) and Bhowali, which are climatically as pleasant as Nainital, and are much quieter

and more to the taste of people who like to be far from
the maddening crowd. Other lakes, Bhim Tal, Sat Tal and
Naukuchiya Tal, are close to   Nainital.

## Ranikhet

Ranikhet owes its present day importance  to the fact
that it is the headquarters of the Kumaon Regimental
Centre. The centre moved to Ranikhet from Agra in 1948
when the British Army vacated the barracks. Ranikhet is
definitely the most beautiful town in Kumaon, with old
style colonial bungalows with names like Windy Haugh,
Trevone, Clyde Bank, St. Albans and the Priory, nestling
in the midst of thick pine and deodar forests. The town
owes its name to a Katyuri queen, who lived in the Katyuri
capital of Dwarahat but loved this place so much that she
came and camped here at regular intervals, somewhere
near the present Ranikhet club.

During the Nepalese occupation of Kumaon, a decisive
battle was fought here between the Gorkha  Army of  Sardar
Angad and the British Army led by Col. E. Gardner at
Kumupur, now identified as being above the present site
of the Military Hospital. A heavily outnumbered Gorkha
army lost this battle as well as a later one at Katarmal
near Almora. Thus Kumaon fell to the British.

The town of Ranikhet, however, owes its existence to
Norman Troupe, an English adventurer, who bought land
and settled down in the area which now houses the
administrative block of the Kumaon Regimental Centre. There
is a local belief that he initially settled down in an area a little
away from where the bazaar is now situated, but one day
he happened to play host to two officers of the British
Army, who were travelling over the hills looking for an
area where a cantonment could be established. Guided by
their conversation, he quickly bought up the area above
what is now the SDM's court, where he planted tea and

had a thriving tea garden all along the surrounding slopes. In 1825 the British Government officially decided to build a cantonment for British soldiers, where they could recuperate from the heat  of the Indian summer and the rigours of campaigning in the plains. Of all the sites suggested by the earlier reconnaissance, they decided Troupe's lands were the best and they were purchased from him. He himself shifted to Holm Farm, which still stands and is now a Heritage Hotel. The Cantonment Board was then set up in 1869. Expanding population and construction has cluttered up the old Sadar Bazar, but most of the old bungalows constructed by the British still exist, though in a slightly decrepit condition. There are eleven old churches in the town, of which three are still in use as churches. Two of them house shawl centres established by the Army Welfare Centre, and some are put to other uses by the army. A beautiful little Wesleyan chapel along the bridle path that leads from the Military Hospital is unfortunately crumbling, but the others are still in a good state of repair

Two very famous temples in Ranikhet are the Jhula Devi temple on the road linking Mall Road to Chaubattia and the Kalika temple in the hamlet of Kalika just above the Golf Course on the road to Almora. The former is ringed around with millions of bells donated by grateful worshippers, and is supposed to be visited at regular intervals by a tiger who is visible only to the priest. Since Ranikhet is above the tiger line, this is unlikely, but there are panthers in the heavy jungles surrounding the temple and it could be one of those. Kalika Devi is the patron deity of  the Kumaon Regiment, whose soldiers go into battle shouting 'Kalika Mata ki Jai' and this temple too, though slightly outside the town, attracts several devotees.

There are other places to be visited in Ranikhet — the Government orchard in Chaubattia, the golf course, the museum of the, Kumaon Regimental Centre, Haira Khan temple, and so on, but the main charm of the town is in its ambience, in the pine and oak-shaded walks and in the magnificent mountain view, which is the most extensive to be seen from inside any town in the country.

The mountain view from Ranikhet is perhaps the most magnificent from any town in the world. It stretches from the Nepal mountains of Panchuli and beyond to Bandar Punch, the Kedar peak, Nilkanth (which surmounts Badrinath), and Kamet (25,447 feet) on the Tibet border. But the central glories of this wall of mountains are Trisul (23,406 feet), Nanda Devi (25,,660 feet) and their attendant ridges, and lesser mountains such as Trisul east, Nada Kot, Nanda Khat and Nandakna. Only 80 to 100 kms. away as the crow flies, the view from Ranikhet (also from Binsar and Mukhteshwar), dazzling white, gold or rose pink depending on the time of the day, is one of the most beautiful sights ever seen.

The best period for the view of the peaks, is from Otober to April, when it can be seen for a large part of the day, except on cloudy days. Summer visitors are always disappointed as a dusk haze masks the peaks most of the time, as do the huge black clouds of the rainy season.

Kausani, where people go for the view, is only 50 km. away from Trisul, but the sweep of the view is not so extensive.

Tourists who visit Ranikhet are very often 'trippers' who get to 'do' the town on their way from Almora to Naini Tal, or vice versa. They usually visit Upat, one of the prettiest golf courses in the country and, if there is time, they are taken to Chaubattia gardens, the government apple orchard. But such a brief visit does not give them any time to absorb the atmosphere of this enchanting hill station. Apart from these two places, Ranikhet offers tourists quite a number of other attractions. Bhalu Dam, which provides the town's water supply, is a good walk, and also has some good fishing. Kalika temple, as has been mentioned earlier, is very close to the golf course, while Jhula Devi temple and the Ram Mandir are on the way to Chaubattia. Haira Khan temple in Chilinaula is a magnificent marble edifice, imposing alike for its construction and its impressive Himalayan view in the right season. The KRC museum which houses the trophies of the regiment is also worth seeing.

## Dwarahat

Within easy reach of Ranikhet is Dwarahat, which was the original capital of the Katyuri kings. Its present claim to fame rests in the sixty odd temples here which have been built by them. Many of the temples are in ruins and very few of them have idols, but the carving and workmanship still is exquisite.

According to legend, celestial deities had decided to establish Dwarka in the site now occupied by Dwarahat. For this purpose, the two rivers, Kosi and Ramganga, were supposed to meet here and create a suitable site. The Gagas river asked a silk cotton tree to wait for the Ramganga river and tell her to halt at Dwarahat till the Kosi joined her. But the tree fell asleep, and by the time she awoke, the Ramganga had passed the area and was unable to return. The opportunity escaped and Dwarahat remained what it was.

Just above Dwarahat is the mountain of Dunagiri, surmounted by the temple of the goddess Vaishnavi. It is highly venerated in the area and owes its sanctity to the fact that when Hanuman flew overhead, carrying the mountain on which the herb *Sanjivini* grew in order to restore the wounded Laxman to consciousness, a bit of the herb fell on Dunagiri. It turned the iron sickle of a grass-cutter working there to gold. A large number of medicinal plants and herbs are still found here.

## Almora

The town of Almora was established as the capital of the
Chand kingdom primarily because it was central and easier
to approach than Champawat. Of course, there is a legend
attached to the place. In 1560, King Kalyan Chand went
on a hunting expedition to the hills of Almora and saw a
hare which, entering into the precincts of the village, turned
into a tiger. His soothsayers convinced him that this was
a good omen, and the construction of the town was begun.
An iron rod was thrust into the ground which pierced the
head of Shesh Nag, on whose head the world rested. But
the King had it pulled out again. His astrologers said that,
thanks to this action, the kingdom would be unstable. The
Kashaya hill, on the crest of which Almora has been built,
has been mentioned in the *Skanda Purana*.

Initially, Almora was called Rajapur. When the British took
over the town, the cantonment was established in the area
called Lalmandi, and the fort became Fort Moira.

Originally the cantonment housed a Gorkha platoon, but
from 1972 onwards it is home to the Naga Regiment, which
is part of the Kumaon Regiment. Though Almora has become
very crowded, some of its ancient buildings are worth seeing.
The post office built in 1905 is a very British construction.
So is the Collectorate which is really the old Almora fort,
Fort Moira. The bazaar is quaint and stone-flagged, and
fortunately only approachable on foot. Within it is the ancient
temple of Nanda Devi, the shifting of which to another site
is supposed to have cost Commissioner Traill to lose his sight.
It was restored when he brought back the temple. Opposite
is the old Shiva temple. Unfortunately, the image in the
Nanda Devi temple is a new one, the old one having been
stolen about thirty years ago.

The old part of the town contains some beautiful old
houses built in *pahari* style, many with roof beams, doors
and windows made of *deodar* wood from the forest at
Jageshwar.

Apart from the old buildings, the bazaar and the fort, the tourist must make it a point to see the Govind Ballabh Pant Museum, which is on the main Mall Road. Though small, it houses an exquisite collection of Kumaoni artifacts, sculpture, coins, and examples of traditional arts and crafts.

Very close to the old Almora town stands the Kasar Devi temple on what was formerly called Crank's Ridge, and was a haunt of artists and writers. D.H. Lawrence spent two summers here. It was also visited by Cat Stevens, Bob Dylan and Timothy Leary, who was the father of the hippie movement and thanks to whom it became a centre for hippies in the 1970s.

Binsar is within easy reach of Almora. From 1852 to 1856, it was developed as a capital of Kumaon by Sir Henry Ramsay, who built his summer residence there. It has now been designated a wildlife sanctuary and has some lovely oak forests. The view of the Himalayan range that you get from here is supposed by some to be the best in these hills.

Kausani is also close to Almora, and is one of the prettiest and the most cosmopolitan of the Kumaoni towns. Trisul, the three pronged mountain, is only 50 km. away as the crow flies and the view is well worth seeing. The place is still heavily wooded. The Anashakti Yoga Ashram here was very popular with Mahatma Gandhi, and is still a simple resort where people can stay. Kausani has always been a popular tourist spot, and has been appreciated not only for its impressive view of the mountains but also for its magnificent sunrises and sunsets. It is green and quiet, and is an ideal place for a holiday. Within easy reach of Kausani is Baijnath where, on the confluence of two pretty rivulets, stand a group of magnificent temples. Of these, the temple of Parvati contains an image that many consider the most beautiful in India. Unfortunately, efforts made to steal it have resulted in some damage to the statue.

Jageshwar, popular with the devout because it has a temple to one of the twelve Jyotirlingas, is also an exceedingly beautiful spot as its 100 or more temples nestle in a hollow on the banks of a rippling mountain stream surrounded by a magnificent *deodar* forest, interspersed with rolling grasslands. Once, picnicking on one of these grassy slopes, we saw the exquisite cobra lily along with many other rare plants. Just one kilometre before the main Jageshwar township lies the group of Dandeshwar temples, perhaps not venerated as much as the Jyotirlinga and Mritunjaya temples in the main Jageshwar but undoubtedly unsurpassed for sheer beauty. The stories and legends relating to this temple complex are related in an earlier chapter of this book.

Temples in Kumaon are graded according to the shape of the superstructure of the temple. The Latina *shikara*, for example, was three- or four-sided, the Phamsana was curvilicnear, and the Vallabhishikar is a rectangular temple enshrining  a Shakti image. By the middle of the eighth century, all three types of superstructure were present in Kumaon. The earliest Valabhi shrine, the one devoted to Candika, was to be found in Jageshwar. The Phamsana shrines here have two-tiered roofs, but the Latina *shikara* was the last to appear. The average European, however, described the Kumaoni temple pinnacles as the Turk's cap style.

## Pithoragarh

Pithoragarh, set deep in the mountains on the border of Kumaon with Nepal and Tibet, has developed tremendously in recent years after the Chinese war in 1962 and has opened up the interiors of Kumaon and Garhwal to modern transport and communication. It is a sprawling township in what was originally a very green valley but which, in recent years, has yielded much of its foliage and green cover to the exigencies of a modern town.

Barron  describes his first visit to Pithoragarh, in 1844, thus:

> The first view of Petoragarh is striking; in one instant when you reach the top of the pass which overlooks it, a wide valley bursts on the view, with the small neat military cantonment, farms and scattered villages, and meandering streams which distribute fertility to thousands of well cultivated fields.[32]

Pithoragarh is situated at a height of 1615 metres, and is 151 km. from the railhead at Tanakpur, and 212 km. from Kathgodam railhead.

There are several interesting temples in and around the town, and Pithoragarh is only 77 km. from Gangolihat, which is near the famous Patal Bhuwaneshwar caves. These consist of limestone caves, the walls of which have been carved into several interesting shapes because of the action of water. The devout see many scenes from ancient mythology depicted on these walls. One legend maintains that an underground passageway leads from the caves to the famous Jyotirling in the Mahakaleshwar temple in Ujjain. This is geologically unlikely because the type of limestone in this region does not lend itself to deep cave formation, but it is an interesting thought.

Berinag and Chaukori are old tea estates, now famous for their mountain views. Also near Pithoragarh are Lohaghat and Narayanswami *ashram*.

## Champawat

Champawat was the ancient seat of the Chand *rajas* and, though off the beaten track, is now being frequented by tourists.

Bageshwar is a town of historical and commercial importance, well-known for its annual Uttarayani fair. It lies on the route to Pindari glacier and has recently been made the headquarters of  a separate district.

## Corbett National Park

The Corbett National Park, set up in 1936, was the first national park in the country and was originally called The Hailey National Park, after Sir Malcolm Hailey, the Governor of the United Provinces who took a great deal of interest in its development. After independence, it changed names again, first becoming The Ramganga National Park and then The Corbett National Park. This, it must be emphasised, was not to commemorate Corbett the big-game hunter only, but in memory of Corbett the environmentalist  and lover of animals.

This reserve was also the first tiger reserve to come under Project Tiger and, subsequently, many other reserves have come under this scheme.

The main or core area of the Corbett National Park is out of bounds to visitors and tourists, but surrounding this is a buffer zone well-served with rest houses and other facilities for visitors. Tourists can go around the park in jeeps and on elephants provided for them to view the birds and animals. Guides are also provided. Dhikala is the most convenient place in the reserve for people to stay.

The Ramganga river flows through the park, two-thirds of which lies in Pauri Garhwal and one-third in Kumaon. During the monsoon, the area is subjected to extensive flooding and water-logging, and the roads are badly damaged. Also there is usually an overgrowth of wild grasses and foliage, which can make it dangerous for unwary tourists. As a result, the park is closed to the public from the middle of June till November. The winter months are delightful in the reserve, specially rewarding for birdwatchers, while April, May and June are more suitable for large animal watching as the drying up of the grasses ensures a better chance of spotting them.

A heavy *sal* forest covers the reserve, varied with *rohini* and the *karipak* or *meetha neem*, the delightful fragrance of which scents the air as you push through on elephant back. There are also *ber, bael, khair,* and the colourful *dhak, semal* and *amaltas*. Clumps of bamboo and a thick undergrowth serve as good hiding places for animals.

The Park is officially supposed to contain 50 varieties of mammals, 577 of birds and 25 of reptiles, but M. Krishnan, the well-known naturalist who has written the official brochure for the Forest Department of UP feels that the list of reptiles remains incomplete.

The Corbett Park is an ideal tiger reserve, for it contains plenty of game for the tiger (four types of deer, pig and lesser animals), water and ample and thick vegetation. The barbarous practice of tying up game to attract the tiger in order to display it to visitors has been given up after Project Tiger was started, so sightings depend purely on chance. They do occur quite frequently, though you may just be one of the unlucky ones who gets to go round the park on elephant back and have your guide point out the pug marks and the patch of dry leaves and grass, still warm, on which the tiger has been sunbathing, only to slip into the undergrowth on hearing your approach. Sightings are more common when the summer sun has burnt down the vegetation.

As regards the monkey species, the park contains both the redfaced Rhesus monkey and the grey Hanuman or common *langur* with the black face and the long tail.

Panthers also live in the reserve, but the invariable practice of this species is to avoid the tiger area, so they generally remain in the core area. Tigers are always ready to kill those of their smaller cousins who venture to trespass on their terrain. Other animals found here are jungle cat, leopard cat, fishing cat, jackal, the fox and yellow throated marten. Sloth bears are rarely seen.

Wild elephants are in plenty and found everywhere. It is a magnificent sight to see an entire herd wandering on the grasslands and though it is a temptation to go close to them and get a better look at the adorable young ones, this is a temptation that must be avoided as elephants are very quick to anger.

Of the deer family, the park has *chital*, hog deer, barking deer or *muntjac* and *sambhar*. Wild pigs go about in small parties or sounders. Also to be seen are wild boar of enormous size.

Migrant as well as resident birds are in plenty — water birds like the great crested grebe, grey lag and barheaded geese, and several varieties of ducks, storks, sandpipers, plovers and gulls, birds of prey including osprey, peregrine falcon and several varieties of eagle like the pallas fishing eagle and the crested serpent eagle, vultures like the Indian and Himalayan griffon vultures and the Indian white-backed vulture, woodland birds including two varieties of barbet, the crimson breasted and the green, and also the magnificent paradise fly catcher. Besides these, there are the black partridge, bee eaters, shrikes of various kinds and rollers.

The Ramganga river is home to both the crocodile species, the *mugger* and the *gharial,* and to hordes of playful otters.

Tourists to the park must remember to carry comfortable clothing, neutral in colour, and sensible shoes and to abide by the rules of the park for their safety. Walking through the area is forbidden and so is fishing and shooting.

## Trekking in the Kumaon

The Kumaon region is ideal for trekkers, not only for the experienced trekker who will be rewarded with some of the most breathtaking scenery in the world but also for the novice who will find guides in plenty as well as helpful local people, ready with advice and support.

Most of the major tourist towns in Kumaon are within reach of delightful lakes, hill-tops and picnic spots which can be reached not only by car but also, and more pleasurably, by walking along pleasantly wooded bridle paths. All walking trips require you to provide yourself with good comfortable walking shoes and an umbrella or parasol to protect you not only from unexpected showers but from the sun, the rays of which can be strong at these unpolluted heights.

Day trips from Nainital can be made to:

1. Maoma Peak
2. Kilbury
3. Lariya Kanta
4. Deo Patta (The first seven are hill-tops).
5. Camel's Back
6. Snowview
7. Dorothy's Seat
8. Lands End (4 km)
9. Hanumangarhi (2 km)
10. Khurpatal (8 km)

Longer walking trips from Nainital to places like Jeolikote, Ratighat, Ghorakhal, Bhimtal, Naukuchia Tal, etc. are also possible for the enthusiast. The exact routes, preferably by bridle path, can always be ascertained from the local people.

Almora is a centre for many rewarding trips to historically as well as scenically beautiful places. The route to Katarmal takes you over gurgling Kosi, past wooded paths, to the famous Sun Temple. Other trips can be made to the very interesting temple of Golu Devta at Chitai, the popular Kumaoni God who dispenses justice; Shitlakhet to Banari Devi via Pandhar; Kasardevi, the serene and beautiful ridge which has won the hearts of so many tourists including D.H. Lawrence, the famous novelist, and Timothy O'Leary, the father of the hippie movement. There are also fishing centres at Kosi or the small rivers, but it should be checked up from the local people if fishing is allowed in particular places.

Ranikhet has several delightful bridle paths through thick forest, like the one from Ranikhet to Chaubattia, or Holm Farm to Chaubattia, from the military hospital to the State Bank building through a wooded valley and further on to Kalika Temple and the Golf Course; Ranikhet to Dwarahat (a warm route for summer visitors), and so on. Dwarahat is the base for the Dunagiri Temple, a spot which many people love.

From Pithoragarh one can make one-day trips to Dwaj, Mosta Manu, Mahadev Top and Pipalkot.

Ardent trekkers, who are prepared for slightly longer trips, can plan several pleasant treks. For instance, a nice walk of four or five days would be Kathgodam/Nainital/Bhowali to Bhimtal, or Almora/Chitai/Jageshwar and back.

From Ranikhet, Almora or Kausani, a delightful walking tour can take you through Baijnath and Someshwar.

The Manila-Marchula road, emerging at Mohan near Corbett National Park, also makes a good walking trip, as does Garur to Bageshwar.

Pithoragarh is the base for a trip to Gagolighat, Berinag, Askot, Thal and Chaukori. Champawat district now incorporates Meetha Ritha (a place of religious importance for Sikhs) and Mayawati, famous for the Ramakrishna Mission Ashram.

The routes mentioned above are all-weather routes. Distances cannot be accurately given, as the new motor roads, at times impinging on the old bridle paths, have made these unpredictable. But most of the paths mentioned are well-served with tea shops and simple eating places. The K.M.V.N. has rest houses at most crucial places, and there are also the older rest houses, perhaps no longer impeccably maintained but perfectly adequate shelters for night halts.

## High Altitude Trekking

Trekking in the higher altitudes, particularly to the glaciers, requires a certain amount of physical and mental toughness. Any young person in reasonable health can do the trip to Pindari glacier, provided he does not have a breathing or heart problem. The high altitude induces a certain natural breathlessness which can aggravate any natural disability in that direction. Trekkers new to the sport should be amenable to suggestions given by those more experienced in the sport, and by local villagers who, by dint of long familiarity, know what wind and weather signs portend. It is dangerous to wander away from the group or to trek alone when snow or fog mask the route.

Trekkers must be careful to carry with them adequate, light and comfortable clothing, and old and comfortable shoes. In addition, it is essential that they avoid causing damage to the environment. In particular, all rubbish generated by their camp, in the shape of tins, bottles, kitchen waste, etc., should either be buried or carried back.

The most interesting treks are to the glaciers, the most popular of which is the Pindari glacier in Almora. Tourists, domestic as well as foreign, make the trip several times a year, and even groups of school children have done it.

The glacier is 3.5 km. long, and 500m. wide and is situated at a height of 3820 metres (reaching up to 5000m. at the top), and the trip takes 8 to 9 days.

Kafni is another glacier nearby, tourists branching off from the Pindari route at Dwali. It is not as well known as Pindari, but many people find it a more rewarding experience as it is possible to trek a certain distance on the glacier itself, which it is not possible to do on Pindari.

The route to both these glaciers, as well as to
Sundardhunga leads from Haldwani to Almora, Ranikhet,
Song, Loharkhet, Khati and Dwali, before branching off
in several directions. The Namik cluster of glaciers in
Pithoragarh district, Namik, Heeramani and Andra, are
for more adventurous and experienced trekkers.

So also Milam, the largest glacier in this area, requires
that tourists who tackle it should be mentally and physically
fit, as the trip is arduous. The main glacier at 3839 metres
is 19 km. in length and 3 km. in width. Milam and the
other associate glaciers, Ralam, Bogdyar, Mirtoli and
Burfoo, are in the Johar valley once the kingdom of the
Bhotiya Johar Raja. The Goriganga river a major tributary
of the Kali, has its source in this river.

Dharchula *tehsil* in Pithoragarh gives entry to a large
number of trekking routes, including the famous (and very
difficult) one to Kailash Mansarovar in Tibet.

## Cycling in the Kumaon Hills*

Among the many opportunities Kumaon offers to the lover
of nature and the mountains, cycling has a distinctive
quality of its own. India generally offers practically no
facilities to those who wish to adopt the leisurely style of
locomotion that the cycle provides. In Europe, for instance,
there are designated cycle paths which are insulated against
the dangers of road traffic and allow the cyclist to travel
securely in the knowledge that he will not be run down by
one of the monsters of the highway or a speeding sports
car.

Without such facilities and infrastructure in this country,
if one wishes to enjoy the unique pleasures that cycling
offers, one has to choose routes where traffic is relatively

---

* The authors are grateful to their friend R.P. Khosla, an avid cyclist,
  who has traversed all the routes mentioned here and who is
  substantially responsible for this section on cycling.

light, and where the beauty of the surrounding countryside is rewarding enough to make the effort worthwhile.

Cycling in the hills has its own special features. First, you need a good geared bicycle with sturdy brakes to enable you to handle the varying gradients with comfort; such cycles are now easily available in India. Second, you need to have available a choice of routes where there is an occasional passing bus so that the strain of long and steep climbs can be overcome by loading one's bicycle onto it. Fortunately, most areas in the hills are now connected by some sort of bus service. Third, all possible routes invariably pass through areas that are scenically rewarding. Fourth, the climate is generally congenial to the cyclist in the months we recommend for the cycling trips. One must understand that the real joy of cycling lies not in the attainment of a chosen destination by the end of the day, but in the process of slow gentle locomotion which gives you an opportunity to fully absorb the beauty of the surroundings.

Kumaon, with its varied terrain, offers opportunities for cycling in almost all seasons, with the exception of July and August when the rainy season makes any outdoor activity difficult. In winter, the Tarai regions of Kumaon are a pure delight for the cyclist. After reaching Ranikhet with the bicycle loaded on to a bus, one can start one's cycle journey from Ranikhet to Ramnagar, travelling through the pine forests of Tarikhet, on to Bhatronjkhan, till one reaches Mohan, close to the banks of the Kosi river. From Mohan, the road winds its way, rising and falling gently through a beautiful dense forest on the outer fringes of the Corbett National Park till it reaches the town of Ramnagar. From this point, one turns eastwards, travelling past Kaladhungi, where Jim Corbett's museum is located, on to Haldwani. This portion of the route initially runs through Tarai forests and then onward through richly cultivated fields till it reaches Haldwani.

The traffic on the route from Ranikhet is fairly light. In its upper reaches near Ranikhet, it offers beautiful views of the snows, and when one reaches the lower areas stretching from Mohan to Kaladhungi, one is surrounded by dense *sal* and *teak* forests.

Another rewarding route runs from Nainital, past Bhowali and Ramgarh, to Mukteshwar. This route involves rather more climbing and is somewhat more strenuous. The road descends from Nainital to Bhowali, which is at an altitude of 1700 metres. From Bhowali, there is a steady climb to Mukteshwar at a height of 2200 metres. The route from Bhowali is beautifully wooded up to Ramgarh. Beyond Ramgarh, the forest cover is less dense, but one is compensated for this by the dramatic views of the major snow peaks.

As a reward for having laboured up to Mukteshwar, the return journey is comparatively easier, being mostly downhill, passing through orchards of apple and apricot. While this involves considerably less physical exertion, one travels with the snows behind one, and is deprived of the joy of coasting along, looking at the snow peaks before one's eyes. On returning to Bhowali, one can proceed downwards to Garampani on the Ranikhet road up to Khairna bridge. From Khairna, there is a steep climb up to Ranikhet, and it is not worth the physical effort involved in cycling uphill on this section. This portion would be best done by bus.

Ranikhet is a take-off point for at least two alternative routes. The descent to Ramnagar and the Tarai has already been described earlier. An equally attractive route is to coast down from Ranikhet for about twenty kilometres to Kosi, and then proceed along the banks of the Kosi river up to Someshwar. Although the route climbs for a large part of the way, the ascent is gentle enough to be done in a low gear. The route takes one through pine forests and past colourful fields with their standing crops stretching on either side of the river. From Someshwar, there is a somewhat steep climb of about five to seven kilometres to Kausani. The road rises through well-wooded slopes with views of the richly cultivated terraced fields in the valley below.

Your reward on arrival at Kausani is the full beauty of the snows with Trisul dominating the range in front of you, and Nanda Ghunti, Nanda Devi, Chaukhamba, Panchchuli and many others standing in their serried ranks from east to west. ·

From Kausani one needs only to give the cycle its head and it races downhill to Baijnath. Beyond Baijnath, with its thousand-year old temples, the road rises and falls, running along the Gomti river till it reaches Bageshwar. Cycling here is easy and enjoyable. Bageshwar lies at the bottom of the valley, and the roads leading away from here climb steeply towards Chukori, Binsar or Kapkot, and are somewhat too severe to be worth the effort of the recreational cyclist. A better course would be to return to Kausani and cycle back to Kosi. From there, one climbs up to Almora and then cycles down to Khairna.

Alternatively, one can cycle from Almora to Jageshwar. The road runs through the thick pine forests that surround Almora, past Mirthola Ashram and on to Jageshwar with its myriad stone temples standing amongst ancient *deodars*.

All these routes, along with many others in Kumaon, offer a scenery that needs to be lingered over and absorbed with a sense of its uniqueness. With the exception of main roads, such as the Haldwani-Khairna-Ranikhet road or the Bhowali-Khairna-Almora road, traffic is light and poses no real hazard to the cyclist. The distance covered each day is a matter of individual choice. One may cover anything between thirty and sixty kilometres each day, depending upon one's stamina, the gradient and the convenience of the next halting place. One must never forget for a moment that the pleasure of cycling in Kumaon is not the completion of an impressive-sounding number of kilometres each day, but in the freedom from imprisonment inside a car or bus while travelling through the forests, and the opportunities it gives you to stop by the roadside to talk to the villagers at local teashops and in the fields, to watch the birds and to taste the fresh spring water that flows out of the mountains. Cycling on the mountain roads also gives you the opportunity to put away your cares for the time being, to establish a relationship with the natural beauty of the mountains, the forests and the rivers, and to reflect on your own place in the order of nature.

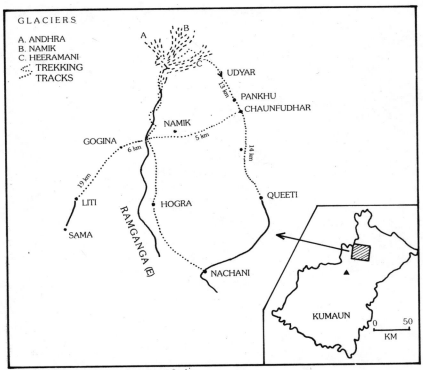

GLACIERS

A. ANDHRA
B. NAMIK
C. HEERAMANI
TREKKING
TRACKS

A

B

C

UDYAR

13 km

PANKHU

CHAUNFUDHAR

NAMIK

GOGINA

5 km

6 km

14 km

19 km

LITI

HOGRA

QUEETI

RAMGANGA (E)

SAMA

NACHANI

KUMAUN

0    50

KM

Namik Glacier: Trekking Tracks. Not to Scale

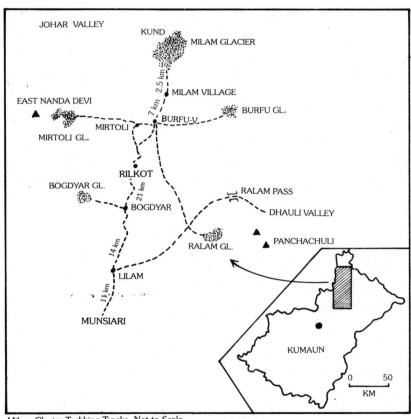

Milam Glacier Trekking Tracks. Not to Scale

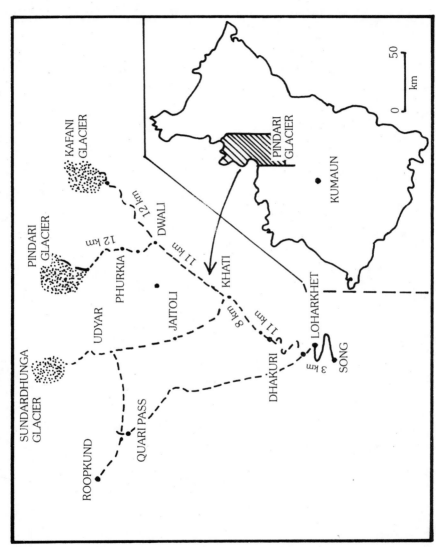

Glaciers: Pindari Routes Trekking. Not to Scale

# Bibliography

1. Aitken, Bill, 1994, *The Nanda Devi Affair*, Penguin Books (India), New Delhi.
2. Aitken, Bill, 1994, *Mountain Delight*, English Book Depot, Dehra Dun.
3. Arya,Trilochan,1992, *Trekking Adventure and Environmental Scenario of Kumaon Himalaya*, Shree Almora Book Depot, Almora.
4. Ashish, Madhav, 1998, *Relating to Reality*, Banyan Books, New Delhi.
5. Atkinson, Edwin. T., 1884, reissued Indian edition 1996, *The Himalayan Gazetteer*, Vols. I to VI, Natraj Publishers, Dehra Dun.
6. Berreman, D. Gerald, 1963, *Hindus of the Himalaya*, University of California Press, Berkeley and Los Angeles.
7. Bond, Ruskin, 1992, *Ganga Descends*, English Book Depot, Dehra Dun.
8. Bond, Ruskin, 1993, *Rain in the Mountains–Notes from the Himalayas*, Penguin Books India Ltd., New Delhi.
9. Bose, S.C., 1972, *Geography of the Himalaya*, National Book Trust, New Delhi.
10. British Council, 1993, *Changing Perspectives of Biodiversity Status in the Himalayas*, British Council Publication, New Delhi.

11. Centre for Science and Environment, 1984-85, *Report on the State of India's Environment*, CSE Publication, New Delhi.
12. Chaddha, S.K., 1989, *Himalayan Ecology*, Ashish Publishing House, New Delhi.
13. Corbett, Jim, 1991, *The Complete Works of Jim Corbett*, Oxford University Press, New Delhi.
14. Dang, Rupin, 1993, *Flowers of the Western Himalaya*, Harper Collins Publishers India, New Delhi.
15. Dhar, U., S.S. Samant and R.S. Rawal, 1996, *Himalaya ki Jaiv Vividhata*, G.B.Pant Institute of Himalayan Environment and Development, Almora.
16. G.B. Pant Institute of Himalayan Environment and Development, 1992, *Action Plan for Himalayas*, Institute Publication, Almora.
17. Guha, Ramachandra, 1989, *The Unquiet Woods– Ecological Changes and Peasant Resistance in Himalaya*, Oxford University Press, New Delhi.
18. Joshi, M.P., S.C. Fanger, and C.W. Brown, 1990, 1992,1994, 2000, *Himalaya–Past and Present*, Vols. I,II,III and IV, Shree Almora Book Depot, Almora.
19. Krishnan, M., undated, *Corbett National Park, Wildlife Preservation Organization*, Forest Department, Government of U.P., Lucknow.
20. Lall, J.S., A.D. Moddie, (Ed), 1983, T*he Himalaya– Aspects of Change*, Oxford University Press, New Delhi.
21. Meade. C.F., 1940, *Approach to the Hills*, John Murray, London.
22. Ministry of Environment and Forests, 1992, *Environment and Development–India`s Approach*, Government of India Publication, New Delhi.
23. Ministry of Environment and Forests, 1997, *State of Forests Reports*, Forest Survey of India, Biennial Series, Dehra Dun.

24. Mitchell, B., 1979, *Geography and Resource Analysis*, Longmans, London.
25. Morgan, J.M., M.D. Morgan, J.H. Wiersma, 1986, *Introduction to Environmental Science*, W.H. Freeman and Company, New York.
26. Negi, S.S., 1990, *Himalayan Forests and Forestry*, Indus Publishing Company, New Delhi.
27. Negi, S.S., 1992, *Himalayan Wildlife–Habitat and Conservation*, Indus Publishing Company, New Delhi.
28. Oakley, E.S., Indian reissue 1990, *Holy Himalaya*, Gyanodaya Prakashan, Nainital.
29. O'Riordan, T., 1971, *Perspectives on Resource Management*, Pion Books, London.
30. Pande, Badri Datt, (translated from Hindi by C.M.Agarwal), 1993, *History of Kumaun*, Vols.I and II, Shree Almora Book Depot, Almora.
31. Pant, S.D., 1935, *The Social Economy of the Himalayans,* George Allen and Unwin, London.
32. Pilgrim (P. Barron), 1844, Indian edition 1990, *Notes of Wandering in Himalayas*, Gyanodaya Prakashan, Nainital.
33. Polunin, Oleg and Adam Stainton, 1987, *Concise Flowers of the Himalaya*, Oxford University Press, New Delhi.
34. Prawal, K.C., 1976, *Valour Triumphs, A History of the Kumaon Regiment*, Thomson Press, New Delhi.
35. Rai, Harish Chandra, 1998, *Hill Tourism–Planning and Development*, Kanishka Publishers, New Delhi.
36. Rajagopalan, V., 1993, *Pandit Govind Ballabh Pant Memorial Lecture III*, G.B.Pant Institute of Himalayan Environment and Development, Almora.
37. Rawat, Ajay. S, 1998, *Biodiversity Conservation in the U.P. Hills: A People's Viewpoint*, Centre for Development Studies, U.P. Academy of Administration, Nainital.

38. Salim Ali, 1949, *Indian Hill Birds*, Oxford University Press, New Delhi.

39. Sanwal, R.D., 1976, *Social Stratification in Rural Kumaon*, Oxford University Press, New Delhi.

40. Singh, J.S. (Ed), 1985, *Environmental Regeneration in Himalaya: Concepts and Strategies*, Gyanodaya Prakashan, Nainital.

41. Sax, William, 1991, *Mountain Goddess–Gender and Politics in a Himalayan Pilgrimage*, Oxford University Press, New Delhi.

42. Shah, S.L., 1986, *Planning and Development of Natural and Human Resources in the Mountains*, Yatan Publications, Delhi.

43. Singh, O.P. (Ed.), 1983, *The Himalaya–Nature, Man and Culture* (with Specific Studies on U.P. Himalaya), Rajesh Publications, New Delhi.

44. Singh, S.K., and P. Nag, 1999, *Tourism and Trekking in Nainital Region*, Concept Publishing House, New Delhi.

45. Smythe, Frank, 1932, Indian edition 1991, *Kamet Conquered*, Natraj Publishers, Dehra Dun.

46. Tiwari, P.C., 1995, *Natural Resources and Sustainable Development in Himalaya*, Shree Almora Book Depot, Almora.

47. Tolia, R.S., 1996, *British Kumaon and Garhwal*, Vol. I and II, Shree Almora Book Depot, Almora.

48. Valdiya, K.S., 1997, *Pandit Govind Ballabh Pant Memorial Lecture-VII*, G.B.Pant Institute of Himalayan Environment and Development, Almora.